FINDING YOUR
*FIN*ANCIAL TYPE

Clearing the Hurdles to
Financial Wellness

FINDING YOUR
*FIN*ANCIAL
TYPE

Clearing the Hurdles to Financial Wellness

CHANTEL **BONNEAU**, CFP™

Advantage®

Published by Advantage, Charleston, South Carolina.
Member of Advantage Media Group.

ADVANTAGE is a registered trademark, and the Advantage colophon is a trademark of Advantage Media Group, Inc.

Printed in the United States of America.

10 9 8 7 6 5 4 3 2 1

ISBN: 978-1-59932-919-2
LCCN: 2018940508

Cover and layout design by Carly Blake.

This publication is designed to provide accurate and authoritative information in regard to the subject matter covered. It is sold with the understanding that the publisher is not engaged in rendering legal, accounting, or other professional services. If legal advice or other expert assistance is required, the services of a competent professional person should be sought.

Advantage Media Group is proud to be a part of the Tree Neutral® program. Tree Neutral offsets the number of trees consumed in the production and printing of this book by taking proactive steps such as planting trees in direct proportion to the number of trees used to print books. To learn more about Tree Neutral, please visit **www.treeneutral.com**.

Advantage Media Group is a publisher of business, self-improvement, and professional development books and online learning. We help entrepreneurs, business leaders, and professionals share their Stories, Passion, and Knowledge to help others Learn & Grow. Do you have a manuscript or book idea that you would like us to consider for publishing? Please visit **advantagefamily.com** or call **1.866.775.1696**.

To my Implementer, Tom.

TABLE OF CONTENTS

Achieve Financial Wellness Based on Who You Are

I t's a persistent malady; the subject of money and finances often brings on a severe cloud of dread. Money insecurities are common, and just thinking about finances can often seem daunting. Financial stress compounds guilt, anxiety is shaded with dollar signs, and financial confidence is low and sinking.

Do you agree? If there was a scale to measure financial weight, most people would dread standing on it, perhaps with even more fear than getting on a body weight scale.

Chances are that if you picked up this book, you've felt the weight of financial anxiety but don't know how to make a plan, much less follow through with one. Self-help books don't apply to your situation. Your best friend's advice doesn't, either. Society simply doesn't approach money from a wellness standpoint.

That's my mission: to part the clouds of dread and help you to achieve financial wellness with a cure filled with calmness.

So, take a deep breath. The coffee is fresh. My office door is open. Let's do this together. But first, I need your attention.

I get it; you've tried this before. Maybe you've tried this a couple of times, each instance leaving you was exhausted and stressed.

Well, I've got some good news. It's going to be different this time. You're the reason I'm writing this book. We'll review some real-life situations and some real-life solutions. Then, we'll start with your story. After all, money matters are a personal thing.

Throughout this book, we'll look at case studies based on real people with real problems[1], and through their stories we'll see what's been holding you back, helping you see how to overcome it.

SCOTT AND KELLY[1]

When Scott and Kelly—both in their thirties—married, they were a goal-oriented couple with a firm grip on their finances. However, in the beginning, they were oblivious to the need for a financial planner.

Kelly, a marketing manager, already had a 401(k) in place, and she was consistently making contributions. Scott, a web designer, spent little time thinking about finances beyond how to pay off his student loans. As they got older, they came to realize that they should take a closer look at their financial planning process.

Initially, they saved some money with success, but eventually those efforts were squandered. They also dabbled with small investment accounts, but eventually became too busy and, frankly, realized they really were not sure what they were doing.

---

1   Names and situations throughout have been changed for privacy.

And so, being a smart, forward-thinking couple who were beginning to consider starting a family after two years of marriage, they sought help from someone who was more educated and experienced as a financial planner to get them to their next, brighter, financially stable chapter. I was that financial planner.

After a year, Scott and Kelly's management of money remained stable. However, they simply couldn't transition past what I call the "Financial Execution Gap," which is the in-between spot where so many well-intentioned people like Scott and Kelly, and perhaps like yourself, become complacent.

For example, how many people join a gym and rarely make it to a workout or a class? Sound familiar? That's money taken off the table and wasted.

Initially, Scott and Kelly had great energy. I was impressed. Though they were intimidated by their credit card and student loan debt, they didn't think they had the kind of big issues that would require the resources of an advisor.

At first, they actively participated, identifying and communicating their goals. They were smart and eager to learn how to be financially purposeful. They said all the right things to move forward. And, with the right promotions at work, they could finally afford to focus on a real future. However, there were always reasons to postpone progress. Vacations came first. Second, Kelly wanted time to conduct her own research—on my recommendation. Then, there was a summer filled with costly out-of-state weddings, followed by Scott's stressful work deadlines. Soon, I simply didn't hear back from them.

It's heartbreaking to see Scott and Kelly's story repeated time and again when financial peace of mind is so attainable.

Once a financial plan is in place, so many other areas of life become more manageable and less stressful. Over the years, I've observed that without the dark cloud of financial anxiety hovering above, even the doubters can focus on other things in life—from relationships to work deadlines—with a clear, unfettered mind.

I wish I could tell you that Scott and Kelly have bought a house and are on track for retirement and confident about their financial plan. But, unfortunately, that's not the case. Like for so many others when it comes to taking action, obstacles got in their way.

Solving money problems and maximizing the solutions for such requires personal planning—a tailored approach that can be defined through five financial types. I call these "FIN types." Discovering your FIN type will make all the difference in achieving financial success. Financial success isn't defined by how much money you have in savings—it all boils down to complete financial wellness. This wellness is as vital as a quarterly massage, your morning yoga class, or a healthy diet. In short, complete financial wellness can be defined in one word: lifestyle.

Wellness, Not Wealth

Poor financial choices and financial illiteracy often result in missed opportunities and a lack of confidence. For example, the number of couples who delay marriage due to financial insecurities is astounding, with 34 percent of people between the ages of twenty-five and thirty-four who have never been married reporting the main reason they're waiting to tie the knot is because they don't feel financially prepared.[2] What a waste of prime years that could have been shared.

But the solution is easy: gaining clarity about what you're trying to accomplish, taking financial ownership, and building a healthy relationship with money will reduce the anxiety that is impeding so many aspects of your life. While money isn't the most important thing in the world, it *is* reflected in most aspects of our lives. Hope is within reach; there is a way to enter into a healthy relationship with our finances.

That's the purpose of this book. It's not to give you a clear-cut path with the "Ten Steps to Take to Have Enough Money to Buy a House." It's not to make sure that you know each of the thousand different options that you can invest in and how you can pay ten cents less on a fee. It's not a rule book with tips and the tricks to financial planning.

This book is about owning who you are and discovering all of your great and unique strengths and weaknesses. It's about building a financial plan that will allow you to execute at the highest likelihood of success. This book will empower you to achieve good financial health just by being yourself.

People carry misunderstandings about financial planning. Some say that regimented financial planning doesn't fit their lifestyle. Those people don't realize that it's easy to approach money in a way that doesn't change who they are. Others believe they have to be wealthy in order to start saving with purpose. That's just not the case. Here's an exciting fact: You can be proactive and build good habits even

---

2   Windy Wang, and Kim Parker, "Record Share of Americans Have Never Married as Values, Economics, and Gender Patterns Change," Pew Research Center, (September 24, 2014): http://www.pewsocialtrends.org/2014/09/24/record-share-of-americans-have-never-married/.

when you have absolutely no money and are starting at ground level.

> *You can be proactive and build good habits even when you have absolutely no money and are starting at ground level.*

This book is for anyone from millennials embarking on their careers, to thirty-somethings looking to buy a new home, to forty-year-olds who want to get more serious about saving—without trying to fit each square-pegged personality into a round hole. Everyone—the millennial, the college graduate, the grad student, the young professional, the single parent, the forty-year-old blue collar worker, or the late-fifties CEO—has a FIN type, or a combination of FIN types, and it's never too late or too early to start working on your financial plan. These identities are the keys to discovering your own unique financial path and to finding your way to financial security.

Once you take ownership of your FIN type, you'll see how much simpler it is to achieve financial wellness and how essential it is to make that wellness part of your self-care routine.

Scott and Kelly were missing something. How about you?

What is a FIN Type?

Your FIN type is who you are financially: the traits that make you uniquely *you*. In understanding how you should approach your finances, we have to look at how you approach the rest of the world. Your approach to money begins with a look into how you function when you make decisions. This determines your FIN type. Once you determine your FIN type, you can be sure you're building, communicating, and executing a plan in a way that aligns with how you best function in other aspects of your life. By focusing on you, you'll utilize your unique strengths and acknowledge and work around your weaknesses.

We can't all follow the same rules to financial planning or we're just setting ourselves up for failure. What I've found in my near-decade as a financial planner is that people fall into one or more of the following FIN types.

- **THE DILIGENT SAVER:** a budgeter who's extremely frugal

- **THE IMPLEMENTER:** a decision-maker and macro-thinker who wants a relevant, narrowed focus and appreciates knowledgeable guidance.

- **THE CAPABLE STUDENT:** a novice when it comes to jargon; one who is fearful of making wrong decisions but is eager to learn.

- **THE HURDLER:** Out of touch with their financial realities, the Hurdler is not numbers oriented. Hurdlers are their own worst enemies when it comes to money.

- **THE ANALYTIC:** a micro-thinker who is data-driven, detail-oriented, and a bit of a control freak

My Philosophy

Once I realized that Scott and Kelly were missing the self-information they needed to succeed, it changed the way I approached other clients and their financial needs, resulting in more informative conversations and, thus, a highly effective planning process.

Throughout my career, I've interviewed more than two thousand people, delving into the way they function in the world to determine the best financial plan for them moving forward. I've seen the benefit to the people who can make changes, who can implement and be clear on their objectives. And I've seen the Scotts and Kellys, who can't. My true passion is helping people to own who they are, to develop a healthy relationship with money that is free of fear and shame, and to feel great about the choices in life, choices that are up to them.

You can't control every circumstance. You can't control the past; for instance, regretting that you didn't attend medical school to become a doctor. If you love being a teacher, most likely you're never going to make $500,000 a year. And even if you're a doctor, you may not have the time to do the due diligence of developing good financial habits, because your workload is enormous. But the clients who find a way to make sound decisions can succeed. That's what is truly inspiring. I love to see people who are changing the trajectory of their financial future.

As for who I am financially, I've always been money-oriented, fascinated with how money works and how it allows things to happen for people, and how poor relationships with money can prevent that. I've been the treasurer in every organization I've joined since the second grade. From building charts to tracking babysitting money to managing the finances for my sorority to making this my career, money has always been an intriguing and healthy part of my life.

I've always viewed money as a reality of life. I consider those beliefs a blessing. I've chosen to learn the language of money, studying economics and accounting in college. I've also seen other people repressed by and about money, because perhaps they've had a bad experience or weren't raised in an environment where money habits were communicated in a healthy way, if at all. Unfortunately, those people put good money habits on the back burner. Like physical health, financial health one of those things you just can't run away from. You are ultimately making a poor decision by not engaging and making a decision about your financial wellness.

I'm glad you made the decision to pick up this book—whatever your FIN type, you've so far accomplished something great: owning up to the fact that there's a better way. So, let's get started.

PART I

Find Your FIN Type

JOHN AND LINDSAY

John and Lindsay are both thirty-one, and about a year ago they decided to cap off their five-year relationship by getting married. John has a great job in sales at a thriving tech company, but with his income being so variable, it's hard to make financial decisions. Lindsay, on the other hand, is a nurse, so her paycheck is a steady, reliable source of income.

The two had some credit card debt because they paid for most of the wedding expenses themselves. They're not "debt people"—it's just that the wedding and moving in together presented a seemingly endless debt-snowball comprised of flowers, venues, new appliances, home repairs, and other home management expenses. With Lindsay's nursing school debt payments, the build-up of credit card debt, and mounting expenses, the burden grew heavier.

So the newlyweds, with their decent jobs but a depressing amount of debt, began questioning their status, asking, "We should feel more financially stable, right? Where was the wrong turn, and how do we go back?"

Unclear about where to start, the couple seemed oblivious to the source of their money problems. In their eyes, they appeared to be thriving. They worked hard, drove nice cars, dined out at fun restaurants, and attended concerts. They thought that they would get a grip on their finances sooner, but it just didn't happen.

Perhaps you can identify with John and Lindsay. You may not know where to start when it comes to money matters—maybe you're ashamed that you don't know where to begin. That's okay.

You've started by picking up this book, recognizing that it's important to know how to interact with money. That's the starting point, and we can begin building a strategy from there, executing the highest likelihood of success based on who you are.

What was your motivation for picking up this book? I'll bet I can answer that.

You've just realized that something is missing. For most people, when it comes to working on a component in your life that's important, whether it's finances or health and fitness, you seek information because you suddenly realize things are not right. In my experience, moving forward in careers and marriage—essentially, life—is often more challenging than you may have previously envisioned. Peer pressure is equally as distracting. With friends and colleagues defining success by the outward activities like great homes, new cars, and exotic vacations, it can be difficult to feel great about your financial position.

Whether you're a CEO or an entry-level employee just starting out, the expenses of life are unrelenting, difficult to understand, and challenging. Financial decisions can be overwhelming. The black hole of searching questions on Google leads to Analysis Paralysis—that Financial Execution Gap mentioned earlier—and it's difficult to find unbiased information online.

At times, you may feel hesitant to actually talk to someone about your finances because you don't know where to start. Many people dread these conversations with the misconception that they're going to have to change and give up aspects of their lifestyle that they enjoy. Many feel defeated and insecure when it comes to decision-making.

If you're in a relationship, you may feel badly that you don't know much about monetary matters, and so you put all of the responsibility on your partner. Maybe you're skilled in accounting and you're expected to have the answers to personal finance, even though that's not your specialty. That can feel overwhelming.

Or perhaps you've tried to do a budget, and perhaps you downloaded a finance app on your phone. Maybe you *have* talked to someone. Perhaps your parent gives you really good advice. Yet it seems hard for you to execute on long-term goals and actually make a dent, despite your good intentions.

What's missing is that you've been taking a generic approach without taking a look at yourself, how you function, and what uniquely matters to you. The most important thing is for you to look to other parts of your life and examine where you've experienced success. Then you can take those experiences and mimic them on the financial front and really approach your financial life based on who you are, matched with how you've succeeded in the past. You can blend the two to achieve financial wellness.

That's what we'll do here: work with your strengths to compensate for acknowledged weaknesses and remove the shackles of your financial fears so you no longer need to walk around in financial shame. By finding your financial type, or FIN type, you'll redefine success as financial well-being, leaving you confident in your plan and clear on your goals and the methods that are going to help you get there. Financial well-being also means giving yourself permission to make mistakes and to realize that your efforts may not always be perfect.

Financial well-being also means giving yourself permission to make mistakes and to realize that your efforts may not always be perfect.

Are you a type-A person—highly competitive, well organized, ambitious, and impatient? That's great. However, one flaw of type-A personalities is that those people are looking for perfection, and financial planning is really about progress. It's an eternal progression. Owning where you are in life and doing what you can as you go is what effective financial planning is all about.

Ultimately, financial health means ensuring that you are reducing anxiety and stress in your financial life so that you can focus on what's important to you. It can't be ignored. Your head can't stay in the sand, so zoom in on your goals. The focus will make you feel confident about your financial planning so that you can get closer to your goals and lower your anxiety level. That's what this is all about: lowering your stress and reaching financial wellness.

How Should You Achieve Financial Wellness?

The first step toward any sort of real progress in your life lies in self-information. The more you understand how you work, what you bring to the table, and what you struggle with, the more progress you can make, because you can build around that.

Just like anything else, whether it's a job or a relationship, if you think about your strengths, you can use those to prop up your financial plan. If you're a good executor and you feel good about the plan, maximize those strengths. If you do really well with data tracking, then you'll want to utilize that for your benefit. If you do better with short-term goals, rewards, and incentives, then focus on that methodology. If you have a hard time making decisions and feel too uninformed to do so, then you need to recognize that and make sure you get someone to find the information you need to confidently make sound decisions.

Next, use those strengths to help build an execution strategy. When it comes to financial planning, so much of how we feel is really about what we're able to act on. So, how do we execute?

Most people would say that what they really want is financial stability, financial confidence, and financial well-being. A lot of people take the first steps to achieve those things, but get stuck in the Execution Gap—but that's because the execution strategies have not worked in the past. They weren't tailored for your personality.

The same philosophy and approach goes for your weaknesses. The more you're aware of those, the more you can focus on how to compensate for them.

When it comes to my own clients who think numerically, I build out a budget with them and work out how much money is and should be in each category—and this works well for them. They have

FINDING YOUR *FINANCIAL* TYPE

a clear concept of how much money comes in and out. Meanwhile, other clients require other avenues, but regardless of methods you use to arrive there, it's all about getting the same answer. Depending on your FIN type, we simply look at your finances through a different lens.

Knowing how to work with your strengths will help remove the shackles of your financial fears. If knowledge is power, then knowledge gained through the lens of how you learn and view things is really powerful. By seeing and experiencing progress in a sustainable way, you can build financial confidence.

You have to look at financial planning as a lifetime progression so that it remains sustainable. Can you agree that giving up dining out for a year will help you pay off your debt? Short-term solutions will not bring about long-term results unless you find a way to keep meeting short-term goals that are sustainable. Your financial wellness should be a lifelong journey, not a quick fix, but, depending on your FIN type, using tactical goals toward bigger goals may be the path for you.

Financial planning can be compared to losing weight for an event, a wedding, for example. In anticipation of a wedding, many people try to give up everything, when that's not sustainable. The moment the big event is over, you're finished, and that goal disappears. While there may be some importance in the short-term, you also have to think about how to maintain that goal—if it is important to you—in the long-term.

MICHAEL

My client, Michael, is single, thirty-four, and has a great job and abundant, variable compensation. Michael has developed a lifestyle that mirrors his successful career, and in doing so he has accumulated credit card debt. He was comfortable with his income, and it seemed that at some point it was going to all work out. But then he reached the ceiling at his job, and it began to seem unlikely that he'd continue making huge jumps in income. In his new management role, a lot of that variable income disappeared. His hope was that maybe down the road the trajectory he had chosen to take would be worthwhile, but his real-time finances began to suffer. He contributed to a 401(k) for a while, but then pulled back on that in reaction to cash flow needs. Life started getting real. Relative to income, he didn't have anything to show for how hard he'd worked up to that point, and he was ashamed because he felt like he should have been further along with his financial goals.

What About You?

Maybe that's you, and all of your friends are progressing at a steady pace. Perhaps you feel ashamed of your bad decisions but keep thinking that one day, after a raise, bonus, or some positive shift in your finances, you'll get your credit cards paid off or get help from an adviser—but that keeps getting put off. That's another example of an extended Financial Execution Gap. You have the best of intentions, but it's just never the right time—then thirteen years of your professional life have passed, and it has never been the right time.

Don't feel like the Lone Ranger. Often, even the most unlikely people—those who have great jobs and the best of intentions—aren't financially sound. In fact, 40 percent of Americans earning $100–

$149,000 a year claim they don't even have $1,000 in savings, while 18 percent haven't saved a single cent.

Financial anxiety isn't discriminatory to gender, race, age, or income. Whether you make $12 an hour or $400K a year, and whether your bad habit is overspending, not saving, or failure to follow through, financial anxiety is real. And unless you really own your situation, you're bound to experience financial stress. It's the lack of action and being unclear on what it takes to accomplish your goals that holds back good people, like you. Good thing you've got me, right?

How to Use This Book

There's no blueprint to financial success, and that's the problem. When people look for a one-size-fits-all solution, what they find is a lot of misfits. Constantly feeling as though you should have reached a certain level of financial responsibility by now is a lot of pressure. Comparing yourself to others gets you nowhere but into a deeper hole of financial shame.

Societal pressure to buy a home, for example, by the time you're thirty leaves people behind and creates fear, insecurity, and lack of confidence, propelling you to inaction because you feel you're already too far behind. The new approach you'll find here is that there is no single blueprint. We need to work with what you have, taking time to understand you and really build a plan that's going to work and achieve what's important to you—not to your friends, your Instagram audience, or anyone else.

At the end of this section, there's a quiz that will help you determine what your FIN type is based on how you approach various other situations in life. Like me (an Implementer as well as an Analytic), you may fall into more than one category. Part 2 of this book is divided into five chapters, each devoted to a particular FIN type, so you can focus on the chapter, or chapters, that pertains to you specifically. If you have a partner, you may also find it helpful to read the chapter that reflects that person, because at the end of the book, we'll talk about relationships and how two different FIN types, or two of the same, can work together—because, as many couples would agree, money is the leading cause of relationship stress.

When you've finished this book, you should walk away with the ability to implement financial wellness into your life plan, the same as you would a monthly massage, healthy foods, or exercise. With your own clear financial path before you, you can be on your way to a life of less stress and shame, and more optimism and sanity.

Imagine that you went to meet with a personal trainer. You communicated that you want to get into better shape, feel more energetic, and lose a few pounds. If they told you that was all possible—all you had to do is train for a marathon—how would you feel? Some of you might agree that's the encouragement you need. For many people, the only running they would intend to do is away from that trainer! Similarly, achieving financial goals won't look the same for everyone. We can continue to compare financial planning to exercise: for some people, getting up at five o'clock in the morning to run three or four miles is the worst thing they could possibly think of, while others relish the opportunity to get that checked off the day's list early on. And many struggle with the thought of yoga, or don't really like group classes, so that would be an excruciating idea, whereas a gym membership would work better for that person's comfort zone. Other people really need a personal trainer; they need the discipline or accountability that keeps them on track—or maybe they need to go to a class or work out with a friend. Still others, just based on what their objectives are, might need more cardiovascular help, whereas some may want to build muscle mass or work on their general fitness level. You have to tailor your strategy so that your goals are achievable and exciting to you.

You know what you like, what motivates you, what sort of encouragement you need, so isn't it crazy to build something as important as your financial life in a generic way? Be thoughtful about your plan and give reverence to the importance of your personality. Think through how you can feel good about your progress and, most importantly, actually make changes that are going to change the trajectory of your financial life and your relationship with money.

Next is a brief overview of each FIN type.

FIN Types

DILIGENT SAVER

As a Diligent Saver, you see things so black and white that you don't necessarily leave room for gray. Saving is important, but what's missing is making sure you're getting the most for what you do. Diligent Savers are numerically focused, and might think similarly to engineers or accountants. For them, everything goes into a box or has a place. They think about saving and security, and they value that more than opportunity.

IMPLEMENTER

The Implementer can follow directions or follow a plan, and they want a narrowed focus. They don't care about all of the options; they want what's relevant to them. They're decision-makers. They appreciate knowledgeable guidance. They are also macro-thinkers, often unable to stay focused on the bigger picture and long-term goals.

CAPABLE STUDENT

The Capable Student is a well-intentioned novice who wants to understand, but who has no natural inclination to understand, financial concepts. They tend to be smart people who normally excel in whatever they do, but financial planning is a different realm. Many Capable Students who achieve in other realms are blank slates in this space. It's not their natural language, but they really want to understand. If they don't understand general concepts, it's going to be hard for them to move forward and really take action. Not knowing what their choices are is probably what's preventing them from making progress—they need to feel a little bit more empowered.

HURDLER

The Hurdler is unconscious of spending or budgeting. They can't fathom how much things cost or how much they spend on a monthly basis. They're out of touch with their financial realities and have trouble defining their long-term goals. And if they do identify goals, they have trouble committing to them, because things always come up. Hurdlers are not numbers oriented and find the thought of crunching numbers to be overwhelming. For Hurdlers, no amount of money is enough. A Hurdler can get a $10,000 raise and still find ways to spend it, veering off track without forethought.

ANALYTIC

The Analytic is data driven; they want control. They are micro-thinkers, often unable to stay focused on the bigger picture and long-term goals. They like to weigh the pros and cons of everything, and they want lots of details before they make a decision.

So, which FIN type are you? Take this quiz, and then use the key that follows to see which FIN type you best fit into.

Quiz

1. **If you wanted to begin a workout plan, what plan would you be most likely to succeed with?**

   a) I would do the same cardio and/or weight routine I usually do.

   b) I would hire a personal trainer to come to my house three times a week.

   c) I would do a thirty-day, step-by-step workout plan.

   d) Before I start anything I would need to figure out why I don't follow-through first before I can commit to a new plan.

   e) Before I start anything I would need to calculate what mixture of exercises would give me maximum results in the minimum time based on my goals

2. **If you had $100,000 given to you to put toward savings, how would you allocate it?**

   a) I would keep it in savings and/or potentially a certificate of deposit (CD) to get a slightly higher return.

   b) I would set a goal for the money and ask a professional for suggestions based on that.

   c) I would need to explore my options before I make a decision; I'm not sure without more details.

   d) I would save it somewhere I cannot access to make sure I don't spend it.

   e) I would research the options available and compare viable risk and return.

3. **What most closely matches your relationship to money?**

   a) I am disciplined at saving each month and keep expenses fairly consistent.

   b) I am good at follow-through—if I set my 401(k) up to save 10 percent it's fine because it just happens for me.

   c) I have a desire to have a good relationship with money, it just seems overwhelming and I don't know where to start.

   d) Honestly, money scares me and causes me stress.

   e) I enjoy the complexities of what I can do with money and the different pros and cons of each option.

4. **How is your monthly budgeting done?**

   a) I know fairly accurately what I spend each month and what I set aside into savings.

   b) I set up automatic payments so that I can make a good decision once, not every month.

   c) I make a good effort to try to track things—I just don't always feel like there is a lot of room to save after spending on the basics.

   d) What budget? Those have never worked for me.

   e) I've built my own spreadsheet and compare the monthly results to an online platform to see if there is any discrepancy.

5. **Why are you taking this survey? What financial change or result are you looking for?**

    a) I know I am saving each month, but I also know that my money could probably be doing more for me.

    b) It is helpful to get some guidance so that I can make educated decisions on my finances.

    c) I want to learn the basics and build a good financial foundation for myself/my family.

    d) I know something needs to change and I'm hoping that this may help.

    e) I am always open to learning more approaches to finance so that I have more information.

6. **How do you plan your vacations?**

    a) I usually travel someplace close by or fly using earned points so I can eliminate or lessen airfare cost. Either way, I never pay for every component of a trip full price.

    b) I love picking a great location or resort and having helpful a concierge or friends make suggestions on good restaurants and activities. It's worth it to have a great, relaxing time.

    c) When I want to travel, I look at some websites and try to find rental houses to cut down on costs and enjoy the destination, too.

    d) Sometimes I go somewhere and make no plans until I get there. Part of the fun is just figuring it out!

    e) I compare hotel prices on different sites. Doing the comparisons myself assures me that I'm getting the best deal once it's all added up (free breakfast, free wifi, parking, etc).

7. **If you invested $100,000 for three years, what choice would you go with at the end of those three years?**

   a) I would get my $100,000 back with a potential upside of 3 percent.

   b) Worst case scenario, I get $75,000 back. Best case scenario, it is worth 140,000 after three years.

   c) Worst case scenario, I get $90,000 back. Best case scenario, it is worth $115,000 after three years.

   d) Instead of investing, I would pay off any debt and then save the rest because that would be more helpful right now.

   e) I would stress-test each option to see the likelihood of each scenario based on current market conditions and associated fees.

8. **If you were to go to a theme park, how would you approach the day?**

   a) I would get there at opening time and plan to stay for the entire day to get the most out of the ticket.

   b) I would look for options to buy a front-of-line pass.

   c) I would ask someone who has gone lately if they have suggestions, and then make the best of it once I get there.

   d) I would get there in the morning and just have fun!

   e) I would find a day that is least likely to be crowded, and I would do my research to find out how to get the most out of the day/cost without unnecessary business.

9. **If you had to spend $100 on something tomorrow what would it be?**
   a) A Costco or AAA membership
   b) A person to come organize your closet or office
   c) New pots and pans
   d) Fun dinner or drinks
   e) An item you have had your eye on for a while such as a tool, watch, blender, etc.

10. **What are your thoughts on meal delivery services?**
    a) I don't think I would ever overpay to have someone prepare food that I can do on my own.
    b) It makes sense for my life to have meals that fit my preferences handled by a meal delivery service.
    c) That sounds great but it's probably not worth the money at this point in time.
    d) I have tried four or five different service companies and have enjoyed them.
    e) It may make sense, but when you average the price per meal I am not sure if you end up ahead if you aren't prone to buying lunch out every day.

11. **If you went on a diet plan, or if you ever have before, what would more likely help you to stick with it?**
    a) A food journal and being forced to track calories is helpful to keep me focused.
    b) I like a rigid plan with rules that are clear such as the Paleo, Whole30, or Atkins diet, or going vegan, etc. That way I know what I can have and what I can't have.
    c) I want to look at the components of a healthy general diet and try to get a balance in my meals.

d) Kicking things into gear with a juicing cleanse or something that is really hard/ out of the norm for me.

e) A certain percentage of food should be in each nutritional category such as carbohydrates, proteins, fats, etc. The body optimally functions based on that.

12. **Which statement sounds the most like you in reference to how your home gets cleaned?**

a) I/we clean it. Who else would do that?

b) I have a housekeeper.

c) I/we clean it; it's not that big of a place anyway.

d) I tidy up when I can and have a housekeeper come every once in a while when it gets a little out of control.

e) If everyone who lives in my house does their part then it is fine.

13. **Which statement reflects you most closely in regard to how you decided on the car insurance you have?**

a) I shopped several reputable companies to see who had the most competitive rate.

b) I have a good plan with above adequate coverage recommended by my property/casualty representative. It is better to have a good plan than to deal with issues later.

c) I have not really changed the plan that I had when my parents helped me put it in place/I first purchased on my own.

d) I am 90 percent sure I paid my last car insurance bill.

e) I looked at the benefits and riders and chose a plan based on the benefits I have a probability/possibility of needing.

IF YOU SCORED MOSTLY:

A, You're a **Diligent Saver**. Go to page 31.

B, You're an **Implementer**. Go to page 47.

C, You're a **Capable Student**. Go to page 65.

D, You're a **Hurdler**. Go to page 87.

E, You're an **Analytic**. Go to page 105.

PART II

Own Your FIN Type

The most important concept is that you own your FIN type: Acknowledge the areas that make you weak. Use your strengths to your advantage. Move beyond the Execution Gap and into sustainable financial wellness.

Flip directly to the chapter that describes you best, or if a couple of different FIN types speak to you (that's normal), examine them both. Read the chapter that your partner falls under, too, or polish off the whole book.

Each chapter delves into how each FIN type executes building a budget, setting goals, making a sustainable plan, learning new habits, and executing a plan. Knowing where you fall and where to go from there is the key to helping you take ownership of your financial health.

The Diligent Saver

You might be a Diligent Saver if you ...

- are very aware of where your money goes

- are great at budgeting

- think frugally

- tend to over-save in cash rather than make strategic decisions

- don't like a lot of help, typically

- are a good saver

As a Diligent Saver, you see things so black and white that you don't necessarily leave room for gray. Saving is important, but what's missing is making sure you're getting the most for what you do. Diligent Savers are also numerically focused and might be engineers or accountants, thinking that everything has its place. They think about saving and security, and they value that more than opportunity.

Diligent Savers love to save cold, hard cash. Usually having collected a lot of money over the course of their lifetimes, Diligent Savers relish the feeling of accumulating savings. But this means they sometimes miss out on a multitude of opportunities, like moderate investing that could generously expand their savings. They see things in black and white: saving is good, spending is bad. A certain amount of money in a savings account might mean more to them from a security standpoint than to someone else. Whether it's $100,000 or $15,000 in cash, having tangible money within their reach really helps ease their anxiety.

If you're a Diligent Saver, you likely have a pretty good idea of your monthly cash flow and aren't prone to having additional, unnecessary costs. You might not mind spending on a high-cost property, but subscribing to a trendy subscription service doesn't make a lot of sense to you. You know that's how your monthly outlay can grow out of control, and you are much too conservative to let that happen.

As a Diligent Saver, you tend to spend more time thinking about how much you're saving, as opposed to what those savings are doing for you. Diligent Savers like the tactical component, as opposed to the strategic component. And with every opportunity, from a financial standpoint, the risk must be worthwhile and guaranteed enough to outweigh the positive feeling you get from achieving a hefty savings account.

Many Diligent Savers are content with the system they already have in place and aren't as open to change as others might be. You tend to think that you can do it all yourself, that outside advice isn't necessary. Diligent Savers might undervalue the strategic component that an outside opinion can provide. And while an occasional splurge isn't uncommon, the Digital Saver calculates every move.

MARCUS AND TARYN

Marcus and Taryn, two of my clients, are married and in the planning stage of pre-retirement. Though they make their decisions together, Marcus handles all of the finances for the most part and drives a lot of the decisions. He's been a really great saver and has done a good job of paying down debt because, as a Diligent Saver, he's highly debt averse. But retirement looms, and the realities of life today mean that Taryn and Marcus could be retired for thirty or forty years, and still stand to face the realities of inflation. So, what they're struggling with now is that they've lived their entire lives being able to buy homes and live well based off of the fact that he's been such a focused saver that he could earn well and out-save market increases. But, at some point, when the contributions and steady income ends, it will be time to take the money that they've been saving and focus on strategy.

But what about when Marcus and Taryn were younger? That's when those traits emerged. In their thirties, they put every dollar toward paying down debt, even focusing on paying down a low-interest car loan when it might have benefitted them more to invest some of those dollars.

Still, their path was better than the alternative, which is ignoring that debt. Ultimately, however, this couple hasn't thought through the opportunity cost of where they were putting money and how they could be building long-term growth.

Compared to Everyone Else

So where do you, as a Diligent Saver, stand in comparison to everyone else? Let's find out.

STRENGTHS

Your budget brings clarity and optimism. You don't spend a lot of time wondering where your money is going. Informed of your current financial state and your cash flow, you're in the minority. So many people lack the basic skills of tracking, measuring, and awareness. Identifying your financial inflow and outflow is a huge, winning factor. You take ownership of your month-to-month financial situation, and that's a positive thing.

Another advantage is that you prioritize saving. You are aware and care that saving and the choices that you make have a long-term impact. You're clear on what you need to do, and you've had a game plan of some sort from day one.

Compared to others, consumer debt makes you uncomfortable. You're really conscious of living within your means, and you're aware of the fact that "coloring outside the lines" can be detrimental to your financial wellbeing. This is a huge advantage compared to other people who are careless with their hard-earned cash.

Another plus: You understand that an emergency fund builds confidence and lowers your anxiety. Unlike daydreamers who think nothing ever goes wrong, you're also slightly more likely than others to understand the value of something like disability insurance, a clear-cut and logical financial protector.

WEAKNESSES

You might focus too much on paying down every form of debt, even if the interest rate is low, potentially sacrificing a match on a 401(k) to pay down a 1 percent interest rate on a car. Or you might pay everything down in cash, which isn't necessarily bad. But if you do the math and compare paying down a very low interest rate debt to getting involved in appropriate investment vehicles you might find that investing or saving the difference over time likely makes more financial sense.

As a Diligent Saver, you see things so black and white that you aren't readily open to understanding all the various tactics and making an informed decision based on holistic financial planning components.

Compared to others, you might be more closed-off to listening to opinions or viewpoints of advisers or people who are professionals in the financial field. Because you see things so clearly in your mind, you might not care to understand someone who has a slightly different take or who wants to help you think differently. These people might push you out of your comfort zone.

Another weakness—you might be slow to make decisions on what to do with the money you've saved. Because you work hard to save every dollar, the weight of those decisions feels heavier. You so strongly value what you've accomplished with your savings that the pain of moving money is worse than the potential happiness of gaining it. For that reason, it might take longer for you to be financially decisive and you may be less eager to implement strategies.

Compared to others, you might underestimate the impact of inflation and therefore neglect to invest. For example, if you spend twenty years saving $100,000 in cash, at the end of the two decades those savings will be worth less due to inflation. Had you invested that same amount with a modest rate of return of 4 or 5 percent, then the value would be much greater after those same twenty years.

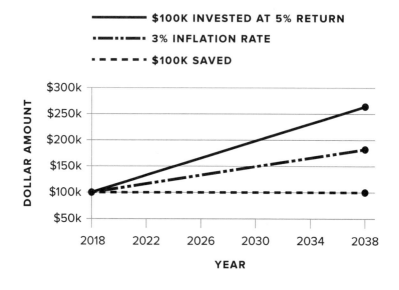

INVESTING VERSUS SAVING

———— $100K INVESTED AT 5% RETURN

·—··—· 3% INFLATION RATE

· — — — · $100K SAVED

Action Steps: Where Does the Diligent Saver Go from Here?

BUDGET

A budget covers what it costs to live your life on a monthly basis. You will find a budget template at the end of each chapter throughout this book. The template is divided into three different categories: (1) fixed expenses, (2) lifestyle expenses, and (3) savings.

As a Diligent Saver, you likely have an excellent grasp on your current financial state. That's a great start. For that reason, creating a budget might be the easiest step for you, because you have probably built this at some level already, or the thought of doing this is somewhat interesting to you. Perhaps you have a budget that just needs a little updating (or tweaking).

Fixed expenses include things like rent or mortgage, medical costs, basic groceries, car payments, student loan payments, phone bills, and car insurance premiums. Those are essentials—none of those expenses are negotiable.

Lifestyle expenses are choices that you make. Your cable TV and dining out habits are among items that define the expenses of your lifestyle. Spending $400 a month on boutique market groceries to feed your family rather than shopping a cheaper option is a lifestyle choice. Joining an expensive gym that costs $200 a month is another lifestyle choice. Clothing, travel, gifts for friends, memberships to home-delivery dining services, and charitable donations are included as well. This kind of spending can be eliminated if needed. (Note: for some people charitable contributions might be a fixed expense, based on preference.)

The last column concerns **savings**. Look at how much you're saving and putting toward your financial plan based on a percentage of your income. Review what percentage of income goes into your savings—this can be a great exercise as you begin thinking more strategically about your plan.

Examine every aspect of your budget. Are you contributing too much into a savings account even though you have an adequate emergency fund? Are you spending more than you thought in any particular area? Think honestly about what you might need to change.

As a Diligent Saver, you probably have a good grasp on comings and goings, since that's one of your strengths, so pat yourself on the back as you do your calculations to see where your money is going. For some, budgeting is the most difficult part of this process. Be confident, because you're doing a good job, and with that confidence you can focus more on strategy and how you can save more effectively.

Realize that positive habits are important, and utilize those good habits. For instance, if you calculate the numbers when you get a raise to understand how much more is going to come into the household, that mindfulness works to your advantage. So while you don't need help understanding the importance of these habits, you do need help with building on them.

SET GOALS AND BUILD A PLAN

Setting financial goals is simple when you have direction. Exercise and build the muscle you need to take your finances to the next level. Don't settle by comparing your strategies with that of your friends.

In order to move beyond the budget, you need to focus on goals. The Diligent Saver does a decent job in the here and now, achieving shorter-term goals that bring peace of mind. For example, Diligent Savers love to have $100,000 in cash, or to pay off a credit card monthly. The challenge here is to think bigger and more deeply about the impact of decisions, as opposed to focusing on task management.

Ideally, you want to build short-term tactical goals and long-term inspiring goals. A tactical goal might be, for example, to plan to pay off your car in two years instead of five, or to save $50,000 in savings as an emergency fund. With tactical goals, make sure you outline a realistic timeline with specific achievements, usually listed in the form of dollar amount. Then try to identify two to five long-term inspiring goals. Push yourself to think as specifically as possible about priorities that are at least two years out. Examples of specific long-term goals might be: purchasing a home in the $400–$500,000 range in four years by putting 20 percent down, or having accumulated $30,000 in your 401(k) by a certain age.

But hold on! Your job isn't complete yet. Planning for both long- and short-term goals is about building habits that allow you to make the best choices that are going to help you accomplish more once you get on the right track.

Once you reach that goal of $50,000, for example, what is that going to allow you to do? What's the next step? Does it leave you with enough cash that you now feel confident enough to start investing because you know you have that buffer? Or, once you pay off your student loan debt, think about what that newly freed up cash flow can help you focus on. As a Diligent Saver, it's important to begin viewing goal-setting as a process. For example, "Once I have $50,000 in my emergency fund, I will shift the monthly contributions I was making to accumulate that toward investments that will help effectively grow my retirement assets."

Design your tactics strategically. Some Diligent Savers say things like, "If I get to retirement and my house is paid off, it'll all be fine." And the only thing that holds them back is that they don't take it to the next level where they will ask themselves, "How much money will I need? What's the most effective way to do this with my money?" There are options that can maximize the work in progress.

Think past the finish line and look at things from different angles, preparing for unexpected changes, such as in your own situation, the economy, medical costs, or life expectancy. You may also find it beneficial to enlist a trusted partner or adviser who will raise questions you may not otherwise consider.

A Diligent Saver tends to be reactive depending on the experiences they've had in life. For example, if a parent ran

Think past the finish line and look at things from different angles, preparing for unexpected changes, such as in your own situation, the economy, medical costs, or life expectancy.

out of money, a Diligent Saver may be more sensitive to ensuring that their house is paid off before retirement, so that they can create security. Be aware that planning is not just about eliminating your fears, but includes thinking about the moments and potentially stressful situations you haven't yet experienced. Consider also other factors that can impact the choices you make relative to how hard you work to save and be prepared.

In building your plan, ask yourself questions and *be honest*. The quality of questions you ask yourself should be deeper in order to effectively drive a plan. Ask yourself: How stressed am I? How much anxiety does financial planning cause me? How much of an emergency fund is enough to instill the confidence I need so that I can start making strategic decisions that have some level of volatility in exchange for opportunity? What feeling or options do I want to have in retirement?

What are your biggest fears about finances? What's your biggest nightmare about the future? What is the best financial decision you've ever made? What is the worst financial decision you've ever made?

Building a plan is going to be more about setting goals, based on the quality of your questions, and digging a little bit deeper than you may have in the past. While you can have a numerical goal, there should be a bigger purpose behind each of those goals.

DEVELOP NEW HABITS

For the Diligent Saver, your new habits need to include, first and foremost, being open to different perspectives. It is not necessary to adopt every perspective you come across, but it would be helpful to be open to hearing them when it comes to financial choices.

Secondly, think about your risk tolerance when it comes to investments. Evaluate the level of risk that you're willing to take in different accounts, such as for a short-term savings account versus a retirement account.

In addition, come to a conclusion about the amount of money you want in an emergency fund. Then you can start doing more opportunistic things with your dollars. Give yourself permission to say, "I have enough cash saved, I've done a good job, it really served its purpose, and now I can be a little bit more effective with these excess dollars."

Be willing to move your numbers around. Diligent Savers love nice, round numbers. A lot of people pick numbers like "$10,000" or "$100,000" to save for no reason other than it sounds nice. For example, many Diligent Savers buy life insurance in $250,000, $500,000, or $1 million increments—not because that's the amount of insurance they need at any level, but because it sounds like a nice, round number.

Finally, take it one step further and seek a professional who can assist you by asking you the right questions. That way, there might be more purpose behind things, and once you feel that confidence and that purpose, then you can probably start making better decisions in the future.

Learning new habits means setting up a new financial environment so you can go from good to great. It's like if you go to the gym regularly and are in pretty fine shape but you want to get to the next level—you don't just have to do five more minutes of cardio; you need to put yourself in a different situation. It might take a lot more work to get a tiny increment better. But if that goal is really important to you, it's worth honoring and giving it your best shot. Put yourself in situations that allow you to go from good to great and build true financial wellness.

FOLLOW-THROUGH

Now it's time to execute and move past that Financial Execution Gap.

When following through to execution, make sure that you are clear on your goals and the "why" behind your goals. Attempt to be okay with building a real plan that works both offensively and defensively. Ask yourself some of the questions that we reviewed earlier, or work with an adviser or professional whose knowledge and skillset you can respect. Maybe have that person ask you questions and share a lens that might be slightly different than your perspective. And don't forget that building slightly more purposeful goals will help boost you over the Financial Execution Gap, too.

Don't just say you need a certain amount of money to retire. Think about cash flow, and about taxable versus tax-free money. Think through the execution results for how your assets will distribute in retirement. Push past the desire to think flatly about your plan. An example flat thinking are comments such as, "If I have X amount of money by retirement, I'll figure it out." Let's be sure to outline our specific goals.

Don't forget to give yourself credit for the really good habits you already have, which is the biggest hurdle for so many. It's commendable that finance is a priority. You'll be able to continue to build a healthy relationship with money if you can take the time to investigate why certain things matter to you. More importantly, imagine how you'll feel when you have accomplished certain financial goals that aren't just tactical.

When executing, make sure that you stay connected to your goals. Always know your next step. Don't tell yourself you have to get to $100,000 before you can breathe a sigh of relief and feel accomplished. If you get $100,000, then what will you do with the money at that point in time? Accept that financial planning is a lifelong series of goals, because when you reach that X amount of savings, your problems don't disappear. You just get to focus on other opportunities.

As a Diligent Saver, you would perform well when directed by a financial adviser that functions as a partner, though you might initially be adverse to seeking help. Because of your nature, you should explore all options, but you might also appreciate someone who is paid for their intellectual capital to help you think through ideas, and then you can choose whether or not to execute. You don't have huge execution problems, but you need someone to help challenge you and make sure you're not missing anything or functioning ineffectively. Consider looking for someone with a fee-based solution. Seek a professional who is well-educated and knowledgeable in their respective field, and view that professional as a partner in this process. Find someone who is willing to explain their rationale, ask questions about you, and understand you. There's value in someone who's willing to take the time to do that.

To get their needs met, Diligent Savers should have goals that allow them to both succeed and continue to challenge themselves going forward, working with a plan that looks at the full context (such as tax implications of decisions), the changing economic environment, and rising medical costs.

Your plan should view your financial landscape from multiple viewpoints, giving you credit where credit is due, setting those goals, accomplishing and feeling good about them, but also knowing that you deserve another layer of strategy. Try inviting a partner to join you, and have them take the quiz to determine their FIN type and then flip to that respective chapter, following up with the closing chapter of the book dedicated to relationships. This kind of knowledge may help you chart a smoother voyage together.

DILIGENT SAVER Budget Template

FIXED EXPENSES	COST
Mortgage/rent	
Property tax	
HOA/maintenance fee	
Home owner's/renter's insurance	
Utilities	
Cell Phone	
Cable/TV/Internet	
Auto payment	
Auto insurance	
Fuel	
Groceries	
Education costs	
Childcare	
Health care costs	
Student loan payments	
Credit card debt payments	
Other debt payments	
Misc.	
Misc.	
Misc.	
TOTAL	

LIFESTYLE EXPENSES	COST
Dining out	
Personal Care	
Clothing/dry cleaning	
Hobbies	
Gym membership costs	

LIFESTYLE EXPENSES CONT'D	COST
Membership services	
Household supplies	
Babysitting	
Travel	
Gifts	
Misc.	
Misc.	
Misc.	
TOTAL	

SAVING/FINANCIAL TOOLS	COST
Contributions to savings account	
529/college accounts	
HSA/FSA/DCA	
Non-qualified investment contributions	
Retirement accounts	
Life insurance	
Disability insurance	
Long-term care insurance	
Misc.	
Misc.	
Misc.	
TOTAL	

TOTAL MONTHLY EXPENSES	COST
Monthly take-home income	
Minus fixed expenses	
Minus lifestyle expenses	
Minus saving expenses	
TOTAL UNALLOCATED DOLLARS	

The Implementer

You might be an Implementer if you ...

- can usually execute and follow a plan when someone gives you one
- like guidance and don't mind asking for help from experts
- want to stay macro, with someone handling the micro details
- value specialists in your life, such as a CPA or personal trainer
- have a job where you manage other people

The Implementer can follow directions or follow a plan. Their focus is narrow. They aren't interested in hearing of options. They desire only what's relevant to them. They're decision-makers. They appreciate knowledgeable guidance. They are also macro thinkers.

GRANT

Grant is an Implementer whom I've advised for a few years. He makes most of the financial decisions for his family. He has a very demanding job overseeing a large department at an entertainment studio, a position that requires late nights and frequent travel. He spends his time meeting deadline after deadline, overseeing numerous projects from execution to completion. His hours aren't nine to five, to say the least. Because of that, the only way he can achieve more is by delegating and overseeing correctly. He can't be the one to deal with every component and, being smart with his time, he delegates to people he trusts.

Several employees report to Grant, so if he's going to get anything accomplished, he understands that he has to ask them questions, find people he trusts, and rely on them to perform to his expectations. This is how Grant operates in most areas of his life, so it's fitting that we mold a financial plan to accommodate his strengths and how he runs his everyday life.

When I met him, we talked a lot about my professional background and his expectations. My approach was to adjust to his personality. The way I could most effectively work with him was to thoroughly understand what systems worked best for him in order to build and maintain a plan. Grant's expectations were not just about having good products and services; he first examined my qualifications to ensure that I was competent enough to guide him in his decision-making. What Grant needed was an answer to these questions: Is this someone I can rely on? Is she going to listen to how I need to be communicated to? Does she understand my need to have clear expectations and that I need to be able to function in a timely manner?

We discussed goals and objectives. Grant's Implementer traits required a more defined set of information for his speed. Implementers like Grant usually have little hesitation in working with partners who assist in executing the most important priorities: taxes, nutrition plans, interior design projects, and, most definitely, financial plans. Implementers are true managers of their lives. Grant is the one managing the vision, while the team that he trusts actually executes it.

Implementers like you and Grant drive the goal. You understand that if you can achieve your goals, spend a bit more time on work and less on the dishes, laundry, and tidying up, then you're going to end up driving in more income than if you clean the house yourself, for example. If you try to do it all yourself, you'll be a jack-of-all-trades and master of none.

Many people are forced to transform into an Implementer mode as their responsibilities increase and their time is reduced. For instance, many doctors tend to be Implementers because they're forced to focus and learn so much about one topic for such a large portion of their lives that they then expect and accept that others have their own specialties, as well. They also view goals on a macro level, hence, the definition of a big thinker with tiny weekly goals might not be as applicable. They need goals that are part of a vision. For example, instead of saving X amount of dollars during a six-month period of time, an Implementer is probably more concerned about whether or not they can afford to send their kids to college or live in a dream home of their own. They back into the goal, starting with a vision and working back to determine what needs to happen to achieve it, as opposed to starting with small tactics that slowly form into goals.

Compared to Everyone Else

There are so many advantages to being an Implementer. Let's identify those strengths and weaknesses and use them to lead the way to financial wellness.

STRENGTHS

On the plus side, if an Implementer discovers good relationships with people they trust, they'll get a lot done. Implementers do a great job of setting goals because they're vision oriented, and so reaching financial goals is easier since accomplishments are clearly defined. Implementers also tend to be decisive. That's great because they don't spend excessive time in the Financial Execution Gap, which is where many people (like Analytics) get stuck, slowing down both their plan and progress.

Another advantage of being an Implementer is that if you are decisive and if you're good at delegating to professionals, then you'll probably have fewer problems in the realm of tax issues. You tend to be current because you enable people around you to help you, and you value their expertise and assistance.

WEAKNESSES

An Implementer's day-to-day scheduling illustrates that they are conscious of making every minute of every day count. Unfortunately, a hectic schedule can push non-urgent, but highly important things like financial planning or getting a will and trust in place to the back burner. It's easy to find an excuse with such a busy schedule. The Implementer's fulltime job is overflowing with workload, unexpected business trips, and interruptions; it's easy to delay and shift financial planning meetings. If scheduling is constantly an issue, getting a good person on your team who can help you to prioritize what's important (like financial planning) could be very beneficial.

If you're an Implementer and your partner is not, you might naturally accept too many responsibilities, even to the point where you feel like you don't really need to include your partner. (For more relationship insight between different FIN types, flip to Part III for the section on relationships.)

Implementers, unlike any other FIN type, might have to slow down at times. They're likely to hear an idea/strategy/concept, get a good feeling, and instantly approve it and move forward without taking a step back to see how that decision might impact their overall financial plan. I see this action impact Implementers in two ways. First, a less financially confident partner might not understand the choices an Implementer makes—even if the choices are great. Second, I have seen many Implementers invest in properties or projects quickly, without consulting the overall plan and holistic strategy for their financial life.

Another challenge for an Implementer is getting proper feedback. From an advisor perspective, Implementers can be one of the easiest types of people to work with because they are clear communicators and are self-driven. If you're an Implementer, you might have found that, because of that, sometimes professionals don't challenge you enough because you're a client that acts more effectively than most. Again, you have to constantly look at things as the dynamic changes—as you make more money, and as there are more complexities, are your professionals keeping up with what they need to be doing and keeping their expectations relative to your goals? Remember, you're good at getting things done and checked off your list, and that's how you can progress quickly if you continue setting and reviewing your goals and keeping your expectations aligned with your vision.

Action Steps: Where Does the Implementer Go from Here?

Start by doing due diligence, double-checking any financial decisions or relationships you currently have. For example, if you hire a bookkeeper for your new startup but then you expand, you should review your relationship occasionally and make sure that everything is still moving along smoothly, ensuring that, as you grow, the help you need can keep up with your growth.

BUDGET

First thing's first: take stock of your current financial state. As any other FIN type would have to do, you must gather all of your assets and liabilities in the form of a balance sheet. If you have a good financial planner to work with, then you should schedule a meeting and bring everything to the table with that person. Have your financial planner compile it all for you—you'll likely work better that way, rather than building your own chart. Performing this task yourself may be a bit mundane for an Implementer.

When it comes to inventory and what goes in and out every month, you can either fill out the budget template at the end of the chapter or work through that with an adviser. It shouldn't take long for a planner to compile if you already have your monthly spending organized. There are numerous apps available for that task. Although you have a rough idea of what it costs to live, an advisor can direct you in planning a more comprehensive outlook.

An Implementer characteristically has systems in place to pay for things in life, e.g., payments made via auto debit. That's okay, but as an Implementer, monitor that those payments stay consistent. With your busy schedule, it can be tempting to let it all ride without realizing that your cable bill has dramatically increased, or that your insurance premiums stopped coming out of your bank account and caused a policy to lapse.

If you don't have a financial planner, you can use the budget sheet in the back of the chapter, but you'll need to block out time on your calendar to walk through that carefully and to make it a priority. Pick a time in your day, week, or weekend when you're the least busy, or the least likely to overbook or get distracted. Once you decide on the best time, put it in your calendar and don't cancel on yourself. This is the part that cannot be skipped, and that's why it's your first action step.

When you sit down to budget, break your money down first into the predetermined categories—fixed expenses, lifestyle expenses, and savings—and then into percentages, so you can have a real view of what you're spending. A common mistake for many Implementers is that as income increases, savings fall short. For example, if you've been maximizing your 401(k) contributions since your salary was $100,000 and now you earn $200,000, the percentage saved has been halved relative to income. Viewing your budget based on percentage of income can help keep things in perspective.

SET GOALS AND BUILD A PLAN

As an Implementer, you're great at setting vision goals—we know this, so define the purpose of your actions. What goals are you trying achieve? Once you decide that, we can work backward from your macro vision to some micro ways to implement them.

First, is there anything in the next two years that is imperative to you personally, professionally, or financially? **Go ahead and jot down three short-term goals here:**

1 _____

2 _____

3 _____

Now project two to ten years ahead. Is there anything imperative that you really want to be able to say that you've accomplished? **What are your mid-term goals? What would you like to accomplish in ten years?**

1 _____

2 _____

3 _____

Are there any changes for the long term? Have you examined your future career goals? Are you in the right industry? Are you stressed about anything with regard to your career? Are you satisfied with your home state or would you rather live elsewhere? Are kids a priority? Is funding your kids' education a priority? **Go ahead and get those long-term goals down here, too.**

1 _____

2 _____

3 _____

Examine your short-, mid-, and long-term goals so you can develop conviction around them and relate them back to your larger vision.

GRANT AND CONNELLY

Implementer Grant and his wife, Connelly, have two kids, and they're facing short-term decisions. They want to make sure that they are up to date with retirement and their estate planning. They know that they need to get their living trust in place, get a personalized CPA, and review the allocation and trajectory of their retirement accounts (they have four old 401(k)s that they have not reviewed in the last five years). This couple had the basic tools—401(k)s and a will—in place early on, but then took their eyes off the ball. Since then, their income has increased, their kids were born and have grown older, and basically everything about their lives changed—and, thus, so should their visions and their financial plan.

For their mid-term goals and planning, Grant and Connelly are really focused on college savings as a priority. They are diligent in saving for their children's college and putting money away for those years. They realize that their house is not their forever home; it's good enough for the next few years, but they know that moving eventually is something that's important to them. There's a particular neighborhood they prefer to move into, so the plan is to make that adjustment at some point in the next five to ten years. Long term, they really want to be able to retire by the age of sixty, with Grant's sights set on transitioning into a small consulting role. Grant has set a goal to have a non-traditional retirement, free of working the same crazy hours and traveling several times a month. He desires more control of his time by the time that he is sixty and the kids are out of the house.

CLEAR GOALS AND ANALYSIS

When approaching retirement goals, an Implementer should have a clear goal and then have the analysis done. Grant is encouraged about having completed that process. How on track are you? In reality, what would need to change in order to get in line with your goals? Remember, your financial adviser or trusted partner can advise you based on your cash flow and can customize solutions and based on your current situation.

For example, perhaps you're determined to save $20,000 annually to reach a goal, but right now you don't have that much to save every year. Don't set yourself up for failure. Envision a modest, reachable goal. If you can more feasibly save $7,000 this year, then that's where you need to start. The key to financial planning with any FIN type is that you have to start somewhere. Implementers generally have all the nuts and bolts and know what's going on; they know that the information going into any sort of analysis is correct, which is why the budget step is so important. If you, as an Implementer, don't feel like that's clear, it's going to be hard for you to make an educated decision and do what you do best, which is taking action and executing on that gap.

Remember, if you start falling behind on day one, it can detrimental to the rest of the process. In a world that competes for your attention, finding the time on the calendar to focus on a goal and honoring that time slot is key. If financial wellness is important to you, make sure your actions and attention demonstrate that.

If financial wellness is important to you, make sure your actions and attention demonstrate that.

Whatever you do, don't procrastinate for three months, six months, or even a year. One of the reasons Implementers sometimes push things off is because they realize the capacity it takes to get something important done correctly. Many Implementers don't want to take the first step to sit down with an advisor or review their accounts because once they know something needs to truly change, it will take a lot of work to implement that change. Sometimes, Implementer's aren't sure if they're going to be able to execute and solve a problem perfectly at this particular time, so they keep it on the back burner to be handled sometime "soon," or once another key priority is solved. I would encourage you to not get caught up in the perfection but, instead, to get it on your radar so you can make some progress.

In short, you must have clear goals, accurate information or inventory, clear gap analysis, and a good vision of what you can do about it when building out your financial plan. That's going to be the easiest way to make any stride toward defined goals. Understand that financial planning is not perfection; it is progress. So getting from 61 percent preparedness for retirement and making a decision to get to

73 percent is fantastic progress. Don't delay because you don't think you can get to 100 percent. Progress is the key.

LEARN NEW HABITS

When building healthy, new financial habits, keep in mind that scheduling and keeping meetings is important. Whether you employ an adviser or rely on your own wits, schedule a quarterly, monthly, or semi-annual financial meeting. Put it on your calendar so it doesn't disappear. If you don't carve out that time, as an Implementer you'll get so busy that a year and a half could pass before you realize you still haven't gotten around to it.

Building good habits also requires that you insure that stream-lined systems are in place—whether it's an online platform or a system for monitoring and overseeing what an adviser is doing or what you're doing, you have to feel good about the tools and be able to access your information so that you don't burn time reinventing the wheel or creating your own spreadsheet. You know that there are effective tools out there for you—from apps to end-of-the-year credit card statements. Utilizing them for your benefit is akin to delegating a task to an employee or an assistant. All you have to do is block out time to occasionally review those tools and ensure that everything is ticking along correctly.

With Grant, I had to schedule a meeting to review his paperwork and find his statements. He wasn't going to do it himself, but if we blocked out thirty minutes and I showed up at his office, we could get through everything without a hitch. If I asked him to get me all of those things as soon as possible on his own, I doubt I would have heard from him again.

Most Implementers have everything they need somewhat organized and can speed through this exercise. Again, the only obstacle is honoring and prioritizing that time. Grant's info was all online, so he was able to quickly access it (after a few password resets!) and pass the information on to me so I could pull together a balance sheet and work out what was happening with his and Connelly's cash flow.

If you have an advisor, when it comes to setting up your new environment consider asking for a summary of every meeting you have so you have that record of what you discussed and what you should be addressing next time. Having something that is clear to read enables you, the busy Implementer, to jump in and out of that quick analysis without losing time.

Also, if you don't already have this in proper order, be sure to keep your info all in one place, whether it's a prepared file with all of your important financial documents or a great online system that can store your financial records. It's most helpful for Implementers to have that information online in one clean, clear, accessible spot so you don't have to update it manually, which is time consuming. Your time is precious to you, dear Implementer.

The Implementer can access the percentage to retirement rates by reviewing retirement contributions. Discovering the required spread efforts can reveal a plan to help you achieve success.

Follow-Through

This is where most Implementers—and people in general—get stuck. To avoid getting caught in the Financial Execution Gap for too long, remember to schedule regular reviews as time progresses. If you're working with someone, inform them of the desired time to accomplish your goals and block that time out on your calendar.

If you need help or if you notice you're having trouble executing, decide if the logistics component is what is holding you back. Are you just not getting to the paperwork and process? If so, allow someone to take that legwork off your plate so you can get on with what you do best. You don't have time to fill out a thirty-page paperwork packet? Get help. **The logistics of financial planning should not be the block that interferes with your future financial success.**

You may want to employ auto contributions to ensure it gets done as opposed to a fly-by-the-seat-of-your-pants method. If you accomplish some of those things, you can focus on what's next and stay vision-oriented, because that's the only way you'll be able to keep this as a priority.

Your financial needs will only be achieved if your financial advisor is challenging you in a way that accomplishes your goals. Make sure you are being pushed to your goals. Your financial advisor should be growing with you and your expectations.

To achieve Grant's goals, we met three times a year. A frequent business traveler, Grant communicated best via email. We had healthy conversations with appropriate response times, which always ensured that we were on the same page. I kept the check-in emails to a minimum as I realized that he was a busy Implementer, likely receiving hundreds of emails a day. I know I'll likely hear back from him within two or three days.

I also understood that, as an Implementer, Grant didn't have time to meet in person with each session, but we made a deal to meet once a year in person, with a slightly longer meeting focusing on the big, long-term goals, while the rest of our planning was accomplished over the phone. Setting parameters and understanding his schedule expedited the follow-through process.

When you utilize the services of a financial planner, make sure you're working with professionals who are educated and meet your standards. This person will need to present a narrowed set of information that is relevant to you so you don't wind up spinning your wheels. And then, if you're having problems with keeping your financial plan as a priority, explore fee-based planning, because if you pay for it, you're more likely to keep the appointments on schedule. The process symbolically appears to be connected to your investment of time and money. You might get more long-term results.

FEE-BASED PLANNING

Fee-based planners charge for their time. This can be a valuable way to establish your relationship if you need to have accountability—someone to truly own your planning engagement—and it can act as a reminder of the value of this time for you.

If you'll remember, one of the two FIN types I personally identify with is the Implementer. So, knowing myself, I have applied this approach to my life in other ways. For example, I have a personal trainer who comes to me because it saves me the twenty minutes of driving each way to the gym. It's not that I wouldn't be motivated if she didn't come to me, but it ensures that I honor this priority. I convinced my trainer to make the process more convenient by coming to my location by offering her $10 more an hour for 5:30 a.m. home visits. If it's important to you and it helps you to get it done more effectively and efficiently, then that's a win.

Long-term versus short-term: Remember to set big goals, but it's also important to realize that it's the little steps are what get you to those big goals. It's worthwhile to spend time making very small steps, and then have a good game plan for when you get that bonus or when something is paid off.

Do you strongly identify with the Implementer? Some of you may be natural Implementers, while others have been forced into the Implementer role because the only way to grow is to, at some point, trust enough to be in interdependent relationships and get people around you who can manage a process.

I'm one of those Implementers who was pushed into this role. I usually like to muscle through the work, but had to come to the conclusion that I needed help to get to the next level in several aspects of my life. A few years ago, my husband had to convince me to get a housekeeper, knowing that my work week was too full to take on housework myself, and that I'd be more effective during the week if I delegated those chores to someone else. So now my Saturdays are spent doing other things I really enjoy.

The reality of financial wellness can be your reality, too. It's a revelation—a feeling of confidence—when your finances define who you are and you're okay with that. Owning your strengths and weaknesses results in the best version of *you*. Congratulations! You're one step closer.

IMPLEMENTER Budget Template

FIXED EXPENSES	COST
Mortgage/rent	
Property tax	
HOA/maintenance fee	
Home owner's/renter's insurance	
Utilities	
Cell phone	
Cable/TV/Internet	
Auto payment	
Auto insurance	
Fuel	
Groceries	
Education costs	
Childcare	
Health care costs	
Student loan payments	
Credit card debt payments	
Other debt payments	
Misc.	
Misc.	
Misc.	
TOTAL	

LIFESTYLE EXPENSES	COST
Dining out	
Personal care	
Clothing/dry cleaning	
Hobbies	
Gym membership costs	

LIFESTYLE EXPENSES CONT'D	COST
Membership services	
Household supplies	
Babysitting	
Travel	
Gifts	
Misc.	
Misc.	
Misc.	
TOTAL	

SAVING/FINANCIAL TOOLS	COST
Contributions to savings account	
529/college accounts	
HSA/FSA/DCA	
Non-qualified investment contributions	
Retirement accounts	
Life insurance	
Disability insurance	
Long-term care insurance	
Misc.	
Misc.	
Misc.	
TOTAL	

TOTAL MONTHLY EXPENSES	COST	
Monthly take-home income		
Minus fixed expenses	$	%
Minus lifestyle expenses	$	%
Minus saving expenses	$	%
TOTAL UNALLOCATED DOLLARS		

The Capable Student

You might be a Capable Student if you ...

- have the best of intentions and want to learn financial responsibility—you just don't know where to start

- may have student loans and little discretionary income but you want to make good decisions

- are afraid of making the wrong decisions

- need financial basics in place

- want to learn and understand what you're deciding

- want to build new habits and stay motivated

- are a millennial (many, but not all, millennials fall into this category)

The Capable Student is a well-intentioned financial novice. He or she wants to understand, but has little existing or natural inclination to understand financial concepts. They tend to be smart people who normally excel in whatever they do, but financial planning is a different realm. So, a lot of Capable Students who may be highly skilled professionals are blank slates in this space. It's not their natural language, but they really want to understand. If they don't understand general concepts, it's going to be hard for them to move forward and really take action. Not knowing what their choices are is probably what's preventing them from making progress—they need to feel a little bit more empowered.

KAYLA

Kayla is a millennial who recently finished nursing school and entered into her career. She loves working in the hospital, and can envision her future and life goals. While she has a good rhythm going, now's the perfect time to start making good financial decisions so she can keep making progress, setting actual goals rather than just living day-to-day.

Some of the real conversation she brought to the table was that, before meeting with me, she tried to do research on financial planning. She read a couple of blogs, and even read a few books on the subject. Kayla's been diligent about educating herself, but finances are still just a foreign land to her. Most articles assume she knows the basics. Besides the fact that she began contributing to her retirement plan through her employer, Kayla hasn't taken a lot of action on her goals. Information and opinions vary and prevent her from confidently narrowing down a plan that fits her needs.

Kayla discussed her issues with her parents, however they were perhaps not the best role models. She's hesitant to take complete advice from them. She understands that her situation is different, and that what worked twenty-five years ago may not be as applicable today. Kayla's parents lived in a different culture, when housing was less expensive and cash was the method of payment. They married when they were twenty-two. Kayla is twenty-six, single, and living in a time where credit is prevalent.

Compared to Everyone Else

Let's compare your unique FIN type strengths and weaknesses as a Capable Student and learn how to work with both to help you to achieve financial wellness.

STRENGTHS

Capable Students have many strengths. One of yours is that you have a real desire to make good choices. You really care and have the desire to do the right things. You take the time to try and read good articles or maybe follow money-focused publications online. You want to learn, and that's a trait that is key to financial success for you.

You realize that you need to be doing something about your future, though you may not know exactly what that something is. You're also probably open to a lot of different methods, like phone apps, online platforms, books, or, an adviser—whatever it takes to help you achieve financial security. It just depends on what is offered to you.

Usually, Capable Students are on a nice career trajectory. You probably worked really hard to reach your career goals and have hope for long-term financial achievements.

You're positive in nature, with goals such as owning property, retiring comfortably, and having opportunities to travel. You're trying to find a way to make financial choices part of your lifestyle, as opposed to ignoring the subject.

WEAKNESSES

Your current lifestyle and stage might lack the cash flow required to achieve your goals. Your desire to learn leaves little time for action. As you don't have a lot of experience, it might take a long time to make a simple decision, like increasing your 401(k) by a small percentage.

Since you may be at the beginning of your career or maybe have high student loans, your cash flow may be limited. But saving even just a few more dollars matters. This will make a significant difference over time. Another possible weakness for you as a Capable Student is that you can have tunnel vision, focusing on one or two priorities. For example, many Capable Students only want to focus on paying down student loans, because it feels uncomfortable to have that debt. While reducing debt is generally a good thing, the Capable Student needs to begin thinking about their finances as part of a plan, not just a single focus. Many Capable Students neglect the realities of risk management. A lot of millennials postpone buying a house, having kids, and getting married, and because of this, some of them don't think about the implications of risk management (such as life insurance and disability insurance) and they ignore this part of their plan. In general, the Capable Student wants desperately to have great financial habits and progress, but also wants there to be an easier way rather than truly building a holistic plan. (Spoiler alert: there isn't.)

Action Steps: Where Does the Capable Student Go from Here?

BUDGET

Budgeting is important for everyone, but is particularly essential for a Capable Student. You may not have a mortgage payment or as many fixed expenses, so this is a great place for you to begin to understand how the choices that you make in your financial life have long-term impact. Budgeting will help you work to change and build good habits—and break bad ones. Capable Students benefit by budgeting, which reinforces positive habits and discourages bad ones, creating the ability to make any necessary adjustments.

Take time to work through the budget sheet at the back of this chapter and examine your fixed costs. Take account of impending changes. For instance, do you know if you'll be moving in a year? If so, develop decisions based off of the future budget if it is highly likely. Define which expectations are realistic and sustainable. For example, if you live at home with your parents, you need to prepare a budget based on your current situation and one based on your future when you eventually move out. Include factors like dining out, and base your decisions on whether you can afford to continue the frequency of similar costs after the move.

I've worked with varying clients in situations similar to this: They live with their parents, make $4,000 a month, don't spend money on rent or utilities, and only have $2,000 left at the end of the month. After student loans and car payments, they'll dine out and take trips, at an average cost of $1,000 a month. But, with their own rent to pay, that won't be sustainable. They have to then learn how to break those bad habits of overspending, which can be hard, because no one likes to take a step back in lifestyle.

Honesty is crucial when filling out your budget sheet. Be sure to account for everything from travel and gifts to extracurricular memberships, etc. Defining those expenditures will provide you with an accurate picture of projections for the future.

Examine your cash flow: Look at your paycheck and what's left over after taxes. Then, based on that, calculate your other expenses. What is the reality of that spread? That's where you'll find out how you can make decisions and really dig deeper at those habits, which we'll get to a little later.

Don't assume anything about your habits, and observe your behavior and spending habits in reality. Did you get an expensive coffee this morning? How many times a week do you do that? Are weekends different than weekdays? What do you do for lunch? Do you bring it to work or do you go out? Does your work provide it? How much does it reasonably cost on weekdays? How often do you get takeout? Do you go out to dinner or happy hour? On the weekends, are you going to brunch? Make sure you are working with real numbers so that you can implement change from there.

The reason why I emphasize accuracy here is that a lot of people have no idea how much they spend on dining out, however they'll estimate a drastically lower number than the realistic one. For example, Kayla assumed that dining out was costing her around $300 a month. But, once we calculated, it came to more like $750/

month, and she realized little things like getting $4 to-go coffees most mornings takes up about $100 a month. That was not sustainable for her income. Luckily, Kayla is determined to make better decisions, so she can reach her goals and a life free of financial stress.

DINING OUT: A MONTHLY BREAKDOWN

COFFEE
$4/day x
6x/week
= $100/
month

LUNCH
$10/day x
3x/week
= $120/
month

HAPPY HOUR
1x/week
x $30
= $120/
month

BRUNCH
1x/week
x $25
= $100/
month

TAKE OUT
2x/week
x $20
= $160/
month

NICE DINNER OUT
2x/month
x $75
= $150/
month

Total per month = $750

Set Goals and Build a Plan

Most importantly in building a financial plan, define three distinct sets of goals: short-term, mid-term, and long-term goals.

SHORT-TERM GOALS

You need a short-term goal that focuses on developing a habit of progress in a timeframe of one month to one year. Keep this simple. This goal will be centered around establishing habits and implementing basic ideas, like paying off a credit card, refinancing a student loan, or accumulating $1,000 in your savings account. These should be real, tactical goals to execute immediately in order to get you moving in the right direction. The key to short-term goal-setting is to be able to check some things off of the list early on and build the momentum for completion and financial success. Those measures can be as simple as going through your budget, starting 401(k) contributions, and putting disability insurance in place.

It's important to define clear timelines and numerical clarity for these short-term goals, like checking one thing off the list in thirty days or getting a credit card reduced down to $1,500 in six months. The key is to keeping a clear short-term goal is to build positive habits, so as soon as you accomplish one goal, set another.

What are your short-term goals (think thirty days to one year, max)?

1 _____

2 _____

3 _____

MID-TERM GOALS

Mid-term goals should help you focus on what you desire to accomplish in the next one to three years. For example, getting out of credit card debt, cutting student loans in half, being able to replace a credit card cost with a new car cost in three years. These are broader goals, and they work hand-in-hand with the tactical, short-term goals. Many times, your short-term goals will build up to your mid-term goals. For example, Kayla has $4,000 in credit card debt that she wants to pay off in two years. So a tactical way of doing that is for her to pay it down to $2,700 in six months. The tactical goals lead to the mid-term goals.

Other mid-term goals could include buying a condo by saving X dollars in a brokerage account. Perhaps a cushy emergency fund is the place to start. Set tactical goals for starting the process to reach a defined amount in two years.

What are your mid-term goals to be accomplished in one to three years?

1 _____

2 _____

3 _____

LONG-TERM GOALS

The last set of goals to have in place are long-term goals. This is where you focus on the big things you want in life, like going back to school, owning a home, moving to a new city, getting married, having kids, or helping out your parents financially.

Sometimes, setting long-term goals can be daunting. **It is crucial to remember that you are not committing to anything, but rather starting to set the trajectory for what is ultimately important to you.** Most people struggle with big-picture goals because of the enormity factor. But try to approach those long-term goals by connecting them with and staying focused on tactical, short-term ones to help you get to whatever finishing line you're aiming for.

Maintaining tactical goals is crucial for the Capable Student. Those goals are controllable. As a new and less-experienced Capable Student, it can be uncomfortable and stressful due to your lack of financial experience. Achieving short-term goals will guide you to building financial confidence. Focus on the follow-through and stick to what's important to you. Don't be concerned that your best friend might have very different goals; that's okay. Everyone's different, and everyone has a different hardship or a leg up, so you can't compare yourself to anyone. You might have a friend who has no student loans, and you may be $100,000 deep in student loans. Your friend might have parents who gave them money for a down payment for a house, and if that's not you then it's just a different situation. Remain focused on yourself and your own goals. And keep in mind that, as a Capable Student, long-term vision is crucial, and the mid-term goals and short-term tactics are going to get you moving.

What are your long-term goals?

1 _____

2 _____

3 _____

Another one of Kayla's goals is to have a certain amount of money saved by the time she's thirty, which is a common priority for many people. She also desires to be debt free, so after doing her budget and examining her habits and cash flow, she was able to make a short-term goal of setting up a savings account within thirty days, while her mid-term goal is to save at least $5,000 in eighteen months. Based on her current budget, that's feasible as long as she reduces her dining out expenses. And, if she gets a raise, she knows she'll have to re-examine things and allocate that extra money toward one of her goals.

Remember that every situation is different. Perhaps you're twenty-seven and have $100,000 in student loans. Maybe it's not feasible for you to have that paid off by the time you're thirty. In that case, paying off your student loans would be a long-term goal, while your mid-term goal is to get the $10,000 loan with the highest interest rate paid off by the time you're thirty. Perhaps your short term goal might be to set up an additional auto payment of $200 a month to begin overpaying that loan.

If you're like Kayla and also want to own a home one day, maybe you know reasonably what it's going to cost. In Kayla's hometown, for example, it takes at least $300,000 to buy a property. Even though it's a long-term goal, that doesn't mean she shouldn't start making steps toward that now. Kayla decided to set a mid-term goal of saving $10,000 in two and a half years, to at least make sure she's progressing. As for her short-term goal, that entailed simply putting $100 toward that amount with each paycheck. You see, the goals can all connect.

The key is to define your goals. Many Capable Students struggle with identifying their goals. You realize you should have goals and should be saving. It's OK if your goal is to do your best for now, save, and to be in a good place for when you decide on your tangible goals. Maybe you're in a place where you may be living in a different city in a year or two. Potentially, you aren't sure yet if you want to get married or have a family. Maybe home ownership is not a given for you. That's fine. If you want to provide options for yourself for later on and do the best you can for now, that's perfectly fine. It's better to build good habits and then figure out some of the components of your life so you can make choices when the time is right. The worst thing you can do is to wait until you think you're ready for those big life choices, to hold off until it's all crystal clear. Being responsible and moving toward a financially healthy direction can and should start now. You'll thank yourself when you realize your early actions freed you from unnecessary stress later on.

Be warned, Capable Student: There's a bit of delayed gratification with your long-term goals, and you hate that. It's easy to get discouraged. But that's why the tactical (short-term and mid-term) goals are so important for you, and you have to set a new goal as soon as you accomplish one. You cannot be tempted to give yourself a break, as that defeats the purpose of building good habits. It's important that you build things into your budget that are important to you, within reason, that will give you a good shot of gratification along the way. Examples of potential priorities might include joining a quality gym, or going out to dinner every Friday. Make setting and accomplishing goals while getting to keep the things that are really important to you can make financial progress a fun and rewarding experience.

Accountability is key, so set a time to check in on yourself. For instance, on the first of each month, take twenty minutes to review your progress. Make it a date with yourself at your favorite coffee shop or at your kitchen table and make that a habit that you can look forward to.

Retirement is also an important goal that we have to bring up in discussions about goal setting. Make your life easier and address it from as early an age as possible. The dollars you save in a deferred retirement account while you're young will have a huge impact when you're older. As a Capable Student, you want to understand the fundamentals of financial choices, and if there is a concept to understand, it is this: If you start saving for retirement at age twenty-two versus twenty-five, versus thirty-five, the difference, as you can see below, will be astounding.

THE COST OF WAITING

With every paycheck, whenever possible, get into the habit of putting some amount toward your future. Even if you start small, it still makes a huge difference. I know it can be difficult to justify when you have so many priorities pulling you in different directions. Not everyone has the cash flow or the opportunity to do so, but if you do, even if it's a tiny amount, build in a habit of paying yourself with each paycheck.

So, how do you determine if you have the cash flow to make this happen now? One rule of thumb I suggest to some Capable Students is that your car payment cannot be more than the amount you put toward your retirement. That suggestion should make you think twice before buying an expensive car if you can't also afford to contribute to retirement. Or what about the coffee you buy five days a week? Even holding back on small purchases can help you stay on track. And when you start making more money, you can add to that $20 a week contribution you held back from your daily morning joe or juice to $40 or $100 a week, and then the snowball begins! Building the habit of retirement contributions is key. I meet a lot of great Capable Students who justify that they will make more in the future and will start on good habits then. The problem is that getting started is the hardest part. Most people will not wait five years and then begin contributing thousands of dollars a month to a retirement account—human nature doesn't function that way. Try to begin putting some small amount aside now that you can build on later; the act of increasing is much easier than the act of getting started.

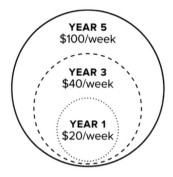

If you're young, you may have no idea what you want in retirement—that's valid, but my recommendation is to just do what you are comfortable with and understand that the more you can save, the better. Over time, you'll determine how much money you really want in retirement, and at least you will be on the right track and not starting from nothing.

Now, Capable Student, I know that you are eager to better understand retirement accounts. Here is your summary: What is the difference between a traditional IRA versus a Roth IRA versus a 401(k) and a 403(b)?

	TRADITIONAL IRA	ROTH IRA	401(K)/403(B)
Tax Status	Pre tax—provides deduction today.	Post tax—provides tax free growth, no deduction today.	Can be listed as either Traditional (most common) or have a Roth option.
So when am I taxed?	Your pretax dollars grow tax deferred which means that the account is not being taxed while it grows. However, it is taxed when you pull the money out after age 59 1/2.	After tax money goes in to the account, and the account grows tax deferred while the account is growing and then the funds can be pulled out for retirement tax free at age 59 1/2.	The same as listed for the IRAs depending on if it is Traditional or Roth. The difference with a 401(k) is that the dollars come directly from your paycheck.
Other considerations	You need to take something called "Required Minimum Distributions" once you are 70 1/2. That means you do have to start taking a specific amount past that age. You cannot leave it in there forever.	There are some other options to access money prior to retirement for certain circumstances, but always be thoughtful before taking money out of accounts meant for retirement. You are stealing from your future self!	You can take loans from most 401(k) or 403(b) accounts. Always evaluate the entire situation before making that decision, but if you do not pay it back you will be taxed on the amount you borrowed and penalized 10 percent.
Can I have this account?	It depends on your income level if you or your spouse has a retirement plan. Don't assume you can get a deduction in an IRA if that is the case.	It depends on your income level.	Yes, if your employer offers one.

- A traditional IRA is pre-tax, meaning it provides a tax deduction today (you deposit the money before you pay taxes on it). With a traditional IRA or 401(k), the dollars grow tax-deferred, which means the account is not being taxed while it grows. But, it will be taxed when you pull money out after age fifty-nine-and-a-half.

- The Roth IRA is post-tax, meaning the money goes in after you've paid taxes on it, so it provides tax-free growth and no deduction today. The account grows tax-deferred, and since you already paid tax on the deposit, the fund can be pulled out for retirement tax-free.

- An IRA is an account you set up yourself (or with an adviser, but not through your job). IRA literally stands for "Individual Retirement Account." The 401(k) or 403(b) which is provided by your employer (if they offer one) can be traditional (which is the most common) or can have a Roth option, so it can be pre-tax or post-tax.

There are some options to access the money prior to retirement, but to the best of your ability, don't do that—don't steal from your future. The key to retirement is this: You have to look at what you're allowed to contribute based on your income. It is best to consult an accountant or a CPA or the IRS website to make sure you can contribute based on your income and the IRS rules.

Do some research, but make a plan that's suited to your goals, being careful not to take generic advice. Maybe a Roth IRA isn't suited to your goals; for example, if you plan to make $200,000 by the time you're thirty, maybe a Roth IRA doesn't make as much sense because you'll be phased out of that due to the income limits. The point here is to build a plan, and to contribute to that plan based on your unique situation.

LEARN NEW HABITS

Many Capable Students confer with friends or coworkers who seem intelligent regarding financial planning. Are they contributing the maximum to retirement? Are they trying to buy a home? Do they invest in stocks?—again, please try not to compare yourself to anyone else. Each situation comes with a different set of circumstances and, often, what you view as successful financial planning has some underlying secrets. They may appear to live the wealthy lifestyle, however you don't know their circumstances. They could very well be in debt or may have money coming in from other sources. It's like dieting—we all have that friend who can eat whatever they want, whereas you may have to work out every day and count calories to stay on track with your weight.

Research. Capable Students often get lost in the black hole of online research. Just make sure that you are looking at trusted, factual sources and try not to take everything you read as fact. If you read something that says to always do a certain thing, it might be misleading, so take everything with a grain of salt. If it sounds biased, it probably is. Nothing is flawless when it comes to any financial tool. Make sure you understand the pros and cons, and do your best to gain what you need from the information without getting too far gone in the Google maze.

The best place to start when it comes to DIY research is with your specific goals, working from there to build around it. If your goals are clear, you can fine-tune your plan to achieve those goals. For example, I work with several resident doctors as clients. Some attempt set up a Roth IRA and they work hard to save a little bit of money there. Saving is always better than not saving, but if they set that up in their third year of residency then they're going to go over the Roth limit as soon as they're done with their residency program; it's not a strategy that can work for them long-term. It's better than not saving, but it's important to make decisions based on your realities and your goals. You can read a lot about how Roth IRAs are great because they give you tax-free growth, but if it's not a strategy you can implement into a plan, then it is not reflective of you.

Follow-Through

Kayla is diligently following through with her short-term goals. She knows that to get rid of credit card debt by the end of next year, she needs to take $150 from her $300 of cash flow every month to pay that debt down.

For your follow-through, perhaps you need an accountability partner, whether that's your spouse or a friend or a financial adviser. Because if you have accountability, as a Capable Student, say it out loud—it's more likely to come to fruition and get you past the Financial Execution Gap. Externalizing it will help you to prioritize it as a necessary goal. It also helps to keep you motivated in those times when you might be annoyed because your friends are all going to Mexico for the third time this year and you don't understand how they can afford it. If you were to go, you'd have to put it on your credit card, but that doesn't align with your goals right now.

You can also succeed with your follow-through by setting up auto-contributions. What I appreciate about auto-contributions is that you make the decision once, and then you don't have to force yourself to make the best decision every week or every month. If you know you want to pay $200 more toward your credit card, for instance, set up autopay on a date that works best for you.

Be careful about staying in the research phase for too long. It's not uncommon for Capable Students to stay in that phase longer than any other step, potentially for two, five, or seven years, because you never feel like you have enough information. You want to make informed decisions, but unless you're going to get a Certified Financial Planner credential, you're never going to feel like you understand every component of financial planning. Instead, break down your goals, learn some basics, and make sure you're researching according to your needs—not just general information. If it's helpful, build a relationship with an adviser just to make sure they understand the way you want to set goals and they can help educate you accordingly. Make sure your goals align with how their method works—just explain to that person with total transparency the level of accountability and education you need and want. At this point, you probably just need someone to send you in the right direction and can make sure you're focusing on the right information.

When setting up your new environment, make sure you have that follow-through on your goals, a dedicated time to review it, and be careful to never leave a goal undone. Have a tracking system in place. I recommend a website that auto-tracks, a dedicated meeting with yourself once a month, or a regular meeting with an adviser to review your progress and set the next goal. You have to build that financial confidence, and that really comes through making good decisions over and over again. Once that begins, you're already on your way to having the financial self-esteem you need to reach your goals.

Do you think you might identify with more than one FIN-type? Go ahead and check out that chapter, too. Or read up on your partner's FIN type, and then flip to the back for the chapter on relationships.

CAPABLE STUDENT Budget Template

FIXED EXPENSES	COST
Mortgage/rent	
Property tax	
HOA/maintenance fee	
Home owner's/renter's insurance	
Utilities	
Cell phone	
Cable/TV/Internet	
Auto payment	
Auto insurance	
Fuel	
Groceries	
Education costs	
Childcare	
Health care costs	
Student loan payments	
Credit card debt payments	
Other debt payments	
Misc.	
Misc.	
Misc.	
TOTAL	

LIFESTYLE EXPENSES	COST
Dining out	
Personal care	
Clothing/dry cleaning	
Hobbies	
Gym membership costs	

LIFESTYLE EXPENSES CONT'D	COST
Membership services	
Household supplies	
Babysitting	
Travel	
Gifts	
Misc.	
Misc.	
Misc.	
TOTAL	

SAVING/FINANCIAL TOOLS	COST
Contributions to savings account	
529/college accounts	
HSA/FSA/DCA	
Non-qualified investment contributions	
Retirement accounts	
Life insurance	
Disability insurance	
Long-term care insurance	
Misc.	
Misc.	
Misc.	
TOTAL	

TOTAL MONTHLY EXPENSES	COST
Monthly take-home income	
Minus fixed expenses	
Minus lifestyle expenses	
Minus saving expenses	
TOTAL UNALLOCATED DOLLARS	

The Hurdler

You might be a Hurdler if you ...

- feel your financial state is overwhelming

- prefer simple ways to save

- can never find the right time to start being financially disciplined

- have tried various approaches to budgeting but none have stuck

- feel your relationship with money isn't very positive

- tend to have a decent amount of consumer debt

The Hurdler is unconscious of spending or budgeting. They don't really think about how much things cost or how much they spend on a monthly basis. They're out of touch with their financial realities and have trouble committing to what their long-term goals are because things always come up. Hurdlers are not numbers-oriented, and find the thought of crunching numbers to be overwhelming. For Hurdlers, no amount of money is enough. A Hurdler can get a $10,000 raise and will spend it, finding ways to veer off track.

AMBER

Amber is in her late thirties. A single mom, she and her five-year-old son live in a costly city, so life can get expensive, but she makes decent money as a buyer at a fashion retailer. She admittedly makes bad financial decisions. No matter how many promotions she earns, the money is always gone. She always seems to have credit card debt. She's tried apps and budgeting, but nothing sticks for longer than two weeks. If she were dieting, we'd call her a "yo-yo dieter." But since this is finance, we'll call her a Hurdler, because there always seems to be something, a hurdle, holding her back from reaching her goals and obtaining financial wellness.

She possesses enough self-awareness to understand that things could be better and that changes should be made. Money has become a negative thing in her life, and she hates that reality. Thankfully, Amber has the self-information to communicate that and admit she needs someone to pick her up and hold her hand through a financial plan that's right for her.

Amber has made poor decision after poor decision: taking money out of her retirement account, inconsistently contributing to her 401(k), and getting a personal loan to fund a trip several years ago. She's smart enough to know that these are somewhat-obvious mistakes, but to her it seems like there's always something else that comes up or is in the way, making dealing with money is a negative point.

Amber embodies the state of the average Hurdler. Hurdlers

can't point to the places where they went wrong, because they just don't know where the money's gone. They don't have a healthy relationship with money, and they always feel behind.

Hurdlers imagine better futures all the time though, pinpointing a moment when things will surely improve, like when you get that raise or that bonus that will solve everything and, finally, you can start saving and being smart with your money. But when that happens, another hurdle seemingly appears.

Hurdlers understand that, for the amount of work they put in, they don't have enough to show for it, and it creates a lot of shame and negativity. And it's a difficult cycle to get out of, since spending can provide temporary therapy, but it ultimately keeps feeding this unhealthy cycle.

Compared to Everyone Else

How do your strengths and weaknesses compare to other FIN types? Let's have a look.

STRENGTHS

One advantage to being a Hurdler is that when you find a good financial planner or financial partner, you can take literal, tactical advice. You might be so fed up with your current situation that you're more likely to want to make that change, compared to others who don't necessarily feel that urgency. I hope the Hurdler in you, reading this book, feels that urgency to change your situation.

Another positive note is that you possess some self-awareness. You recognize that you don't have good financial habits and so you're more open to suggestions, while other people might be more close-minded, assuming they don't need much help. Admitting that you need help is an important strength.

WEAKNESSES

Some weaknesses include bad spending habits. You don't have the best instincts when it comes to money. You also don't have a very good idea of where your money goes, and you don't naturally follow-through, so you're going to need a little bit of micromanagement when it comes to your financial goals, whereas other people can motivate themselves.

Another weakness is that you tend to be hesitant to communicate or share your goals with other people, so you really need a good support network—whether that's a friend or a family member or a financial adviser. You need that discipline *and* the support to keep your goals top-of-mind.

You also have to get over the fact that it's never going to be the right time to start building financial discipline—not even when your kids are out of preschool and they can go to kindergarten for free. That money will probably be immediately reallocated. Because when they're done with preschool, the next thing is gymnastics or soccer or after-school care. There's always something.

Action Steps: Where Does the Hurdler Go from Here?

BUDGET

The first step is to review your expenses, take inventory, and make a budget—this is where you, as a Hurdler, start to lose momentum (I know you were about to put this book down!), so be careful here.

As soon as you have to do exercises like this, you tend to throw your arms up in despair, assuming this will never help you. So, stay open minded, and have a little more faith in yourself and in the process.

The reality is that during this step you must dig a little. One of the Hurdler's big challenges is "the missing money"— that sum of cash that mysteriously disappears from your account each month. The culprit can be anything and everything from that morning coffee you grab on the way to work, to subscriptions that are auto-debited from your account. These things add up, and working through the details of where you've spent all of this money can be a reality you want to put off facing. But filling out the budget sheet at the back of the chapter is essential—so take the time and sit down and go through it, ideally with a partner or someone you trust.

Gather your credit card statements and go through and fill out each component with as much accuracy as possible. You may find that there's excess money you can manage better, like shopping money, dry cleaning money, monthly charitable donations, or magazine subscriptions you forgot about and aren't sure how to stop. Analyze your spending closely—without knowing those habits you can't gain clarity, and that'll make it hard for you to make real changes.

The Hurdler should focus on percentages. What percentage of your income goes toward fixed living, lifestyle, savings, and debt reduction? The big key for the Hurdler or anyone with decent debt is that if you're spending 10 to 25 percent of your income servicing debt, it's really difficult to get out of that cycle. You have to acknowledge that and stay focused on the positive as you refocus on that debt. If you get one card paid off, you can reallocate that $200 a month to another one, so it'll create a snowball effect in a positive way.

Keep a firm grip on your cash flow. With debt, find out the real minimums and interest rates so you can make really proactive choices.

As a Hurdler, you should take inventory and focus on all of your percentages, making sure that you do this all in one sitting. If there's one night that it's worth getting a babysitter, it's for this important budgeting session. If you're childless and/or single, sit down and turn the TV off and get a friend or an adviser to help walk you through this so you don't lose heart and quit, and, of course, to keep you accountable. Focus on the task and not the emotion tied to it.

When you sit down to prepare your budget, remember to gather all of your resources including your computer with login information, printed credit card statements, etc. Block off at least an hour to an hour and a half to work through the exercise, using the budget sheet in this book, and find those percentages we talked about earlier. Then do a sweep of your budget and determine if there's anything you can get rid of immediately. For instance, are you drastically overpaying on car insurance? Can you switch to a cheaper dry cleaner? Strike anything that needs to go.

What are the Hurdler's habits when it comes to a budget? Typically, debt tends to increase, but never decrease. You may be in a constant juggle of robbing Peter to pay Paul, transferring funds often, paying down one card but then taking a line of equity out on something else. It's always a juggle—and "juggle" rhymes with "struggle."

SET GOALS AND BUILD A PLAN

For Hurdlers like Amber, setting a big goal and envisioning how reaching that goal is going to make her feel is important to keep her focused. For example, you could pick three or four big-picture goals that are important to you. Amber, for example, wants to build good habits so she can teach her son how to manage his own money, so setting a good example is a priority. She doesn't want to project her anxiety to him. She doesn't want him to have to care for her

Next, make a sixty-day goal. Amber's sixty-day goal was to look at her debt. She was overpaying, rounding everything up. So if the minimum was $173, she was paying $200. The minimum on another card was $91 and she was paying $100. Her student loan was $195, so she was paying $225. Overpaying on debt is good if you can do it, but Amber needed to buckle down and pay minimums on low-interest cards and use the extra cash to pay down the high-interest card. She needs a real debt reduction strategy.

Documenting it helps move you closer to your goal. Write down your sixty-day goal here:

_____

_____

Decide on your ninety-day goal. For Amber, that meant getting that $4,000 high-interest credit card paid down to $2,800. Even though it's not gone, she's set very clear goals on where she should be in an appropriate time frame.

What's your ninety-day goal?

_____

_____

Other Hurdlers' sixty- or ninety-day goals might be to consolidate the four or five little IRAs they have accumulated over time. Another goal may be to substitute your excess magazine subscriptions or a Kindle subscription you're not really using to buy disability insurance. Identify a category of spending that's out of control or unnecessary—like manicures, buying lunch every day, or subscriptions—and apply it somewhere more useful.

Take any unproductive dollars and put them toward your financial plan that's going to help you be more financially stable. Even if you have to allot yourself an envelope of cash with a specific dollar amount you can use for dining out for a month, do what you know will be effective for yourself.

To succeed, the key for Hurdlers is to keep setting new thirty-day goals once one is accomplished—the same goes for your sixty- and ninety-day goals—and to find an accountability partner, since Hurdlers need accountability. These goals should roll along, each thirty days, your old sixty-day goal becomes your new thirty-day goal, and so on.

JANUARY

Thirty-Day Goal: Sign up for the match on 401(k)

Sixty-Day Goal: Use extra cash to pay down high-interest card

Ninety-Day Goal: Consolidate IRAs

FEBRUARY

Thirty-Day Goal: Use extra cash to pay down high-interest card

Sixty-Day Goal: Consolidate IRAs

Ninety-Day Goal: Get rid of unnecessary spending

Hurdlers are often disillusioned about achieving their financial destiny. There's a time and place for the you-only-live-once mentality, but if you have decided to make your financial health a priority, then it is time to start being more considerate about your financial future. Never thinking about tomorrow can be very problematic for you and the people around you. That's why Amber came to me. She knew her decisions would impact her son, and she grew tired of the self-loathing that followed her yo-yo spending and inconsistent effort.

RETIREMENT

The Hurdler needs to understand that the decisions you make now matter in long-term planning for the future. There is never a better time to plan for retirement.

Many people spend around $20/week on coffee. If you put that toward retirement in a deferred account earning 8 percent from age twenty-five to sixty-five, not including inflation (assuming cost of coffee goes up), by age sixty-five you would have $315,000.

As a Hurdler, you should approach retirement with the mentality that some is better than none, and you're going to benefit most from sending money away, out of sight, out of mind. If you have a retirement account that can take money out prior to you ever seeing it, that's probably helpful.

Of great importance for the Hurdler, when making retirement contributions, you can't make that change and continue acquiring more credit card debt to keep financing your life. For example, don't sign up to contribute to your 401(k) and then just rack up more debt! Cease with the excuses for spending, since many Hurdlers tend to be prone to taking from their retirement accounts, despite the penalties. You can't look at retirement as accessible dollars. While there are options for removing money from 401(k)s for emergencies or very particular situations, it can't be your go-to. You need to be able to set up habits and send money away so it's inaccessible—that's your best shot at saving and building sufficient resources for retirement.

If you don't build a plan, it's easy to fall behind. For the Hurdler, it's easy to fall back into old habits and lose motivation, especially if you don't have real accountability systems in place. If you cheat, just know that this puts you at risk of falling behind.

LEARN NEW HABITS

Amber had to work diligently to build new habits, so she started with keeping it simple. Stay simple so that progress is easy to track. Don't take on too many things at once. Success is more in your reach by getting positive reinforcement and good financial self-esteem early on, and that's done with easy-to-reach thirty-day goals.

Making small changes—like when Amber was able to reduce her phone bill and allocate that cash toward debt—can teach you healthy, new habits. Constantly achieving those short-term goals is going to reshape your mentality when it comes to your financial life, changing it from a huge burden to something that's really exciting and under your control.

Learning new habits is all about setting up a new environment for yourself. Amber realized she needed real accountability and she was unwilling ask that of a friend. She was embarrassed to reveal her financially upside-down life, and she wasn't comfortable in communicating that, in-depth, to a lot of her friends. For Amber, it was important to find an adviser who could give unbiased and nonjudgmental guidance and accountability.

She set up her environment in a way that was her best route to success, knowing that if she paid for it she'd get her money's worth and follow through, as opposed to someone who wouldn't hold her as accountable.

Amber also set consequences for failure. If she hit her thirty-day goal, she rewarded herself by keeping her yoga membership for the next month. If she didn't, she had to give it up. She set up carrots and sticks for her environment because she knows that has worked best for her in the past.

Amber's ninety-day goal for paying off the large credit card debt came with a reward on the back end. She promised her son that she would take him ice skating if she achieved the goal, guaranteeing gratification both for herself and her son. If you're serious about your goal, put all of your energy into creating that environment.

Learning the basics is the key to setting up your new environment and building new habits. For example, investing in your 401(k) is kind of like cooking—you don't cook using only one ingredient. Invite a group of friends over for three courses of plain broccoli and you'll likely get some strange looks! Diversification is important. Try to learn concepts through things that are of interest to you or that naturally make a little bit more sense to you.

FOLLOW-THROUGH

"Change happens when the pain of staying the same is greater than the pain of change," says finance guru Tony Robbins. Again, for successful follow-through, remember this: You have to really *want* to make a change. It's easy to stay the same. It's hard to change things, so it has to be important to you. And you have to find an accountability partner to make the follow-through a feasible reality for you. Additionally, remember that you need to make a good decision once and not have to make that good decision every week or every month. Don't put yourself in the position of deciding this month if you want to contribute to your 401(k) or your IRA or overpay that credit card by $50—set up autopay so it happens without the burden of you letting go of that cash. Remember: out of sight, out of mind should be the mantra of the Hurdler.

Follow-through success also relies on making sure you've hit your goals. For example, vow to spend no more than $300 on personal care in the next three months, and only buy (an affordable, $17 or less) lunch out once a week—those are really clear goals.

The Hurdler's highest likelihood of success entails staying energized, open minded, and accountable, rebuilding that financial confidence with the understanding that this is a lifelong journey. Don't think that you can reward yourself and quit after reaching one or two goals—stay motivated by setting a new goal once one is accomplished.

Just like with your health, you're in it for the long run, so take it in stride. Find a partner who won't be hostile toward your financial situation, someone you're comfortable with. If that's an adviser, you may want to look for a fee-based person so you can prioritize financial planning—they're going to be able to give you a little bit more time to walk through all of these exercises and really keep you focused.

To avoid getting stuck in the Financial Execution Gap, don't forget to visualize long-term goals, focusing on the *feeling* of accomplishing them. For example, getting out of credit card debt will teach

Amber's son the right way to manage finances. It keeps him from experiencing the same feelings that she has had as an adult.

Those are great feelings that can get you to follow-through. Achieving your goals give you productivity-fueled adrenaline, and that can be addictive. That's what Hurdlers need to keep going.

If you use a financial adviser, you should plan to meet four times a year, minimum. That can be by phone or in person but you need that accountability to track your progress in reaching your ninety-day goal.

Remember, Hurdler, it's not hopeless. No one is hopeless. It's all going to be okay! You might just have to buckle down and get to work. The longer you delay, the more difficult that reality will be to achieve.

HURDLER Budget Template

FIXED EXPENSES	COST
Mortgage/rent	
Property tax	
HOA/maintenance fee	
Home owner's/renter's insurance	
Utilities	
Cell phone	
Cable/TV/Internet	
Auto payment	
Auto insurance	
Fuel	
Groceries	
Education costs	
Childcare	
Health care costs	
Student loan payments	
Credit card debt payments	
Other debt payments	
Misc.	
Misc.	
Misc.	
TOTAL	

LIFESTYLE EXPENSES	COST
Dining out	
Personal care	
Clothing/dry cleaning	
Hobbies	
Gym membership costs	

LIFESTYLE EXPENSES CONT'D	COST
Membership services	
Household supplies	
Babysitting	
Travel	
Gifts	
Misc.	
Misc.	
Misc.	
TOTAL	

SAVING/FINANCIAL TOOLS	COST
Contributions to savings account	
529/college accounts	
HSA/FSA/DCA	
Non-qualified investment contributions	
Retirement accounts	
Life insurance	
Disability insurance	
Long-term care insurance	
Misc.	
Misc.	
Misc.	
TOTAL	

TOTAL MONTHLY EXPENSES	COST
Monthly take-home income	
Minus fixed expenses	
Minus lifestyle expenses	
Minus saving expenses	
TOTAL UNALLOCATED DOLLARS	

The Analytic

You might be an Analytic if you ...

- love research, but you don't have adequate time for it

- have attempted to create multiple spreadsheets or systems to track things

- tend to keep a lot of excess money in cash holdings because you haven't gotten around to deciding what would be more effective

- are not sitting in the CEO seat of your life—you know you're not directing various aspects of your life effectively

- asking for help is often a struggle

The Analytic is data driven. They want the control. They are micro-thinkers, often unable to stay focused on the bigger picture and long-term goals. They like to weigh the pros and cons of everything, and they want lots of details.

IAN

My client, Ian, is a thirty-six-year-old software engineer who is single, smart, and has continually advanced in his career. He works for a large company and loves his work, which has provided ample opportunities for him. When it comes to his financial life, he's saved wisely, but hasn't progressed much beyond that. Ian is the type of guy who would rather know the internal workings of the watch—what makes the device tick—than the time of day. So rather than deciding on and implementing a good financial plan, he's spent a lot of time thinking through all the possible decisions and options that can make up a plan. Ian's been busy creating different spreadsheets, reading articles, and trying various approaches to financial organization.

At the end of the day, he's not a bad saver—it's just that the Financial Execution Gap keeps widening for him because he gets caught in the analysis phase and complexity of the details. Those things bring him joy. As his job has gotten more demanding, he has less time to focus on these little projects and concepts. Ian stops to think through his choices at length before he can progress and make the best decisions for himself. For example, in his 410(k), he has kept a significant amount in cash for the last two years. He had intentions to invest it once he reviewed different fund choices, but then he wound up with more questions than he started with. Before he knew it, the market had a significant amount of fluctuation, leaving him wondering if it was the right time to invest. He realizes he needs to invest that money, but is stuck in that gap trying to determine the smartest route, so he has not made any progress.

Ian has the best of intentions but hasn't taken a lot of effective action at this point. As an Analytic, it's hard for him because he wants to understand everything about financial decisions, but there's a lot to it. He's been a professional now for almost fifteen years, and realizes that he can't keep sitting on the sidelines waiting for it to be the perfect time for him to know everything about his choices before he buckles down and makes some real decisions.

Compared to Everyone Else

Let's compare your strengths and weaknesses as an Analytic FIN type now so you can make the best of it all.

STRENGTHS

Compared to everyone else, the Analytic has many advantages. Analytics really do care about their financial situations. You want to get things done the right way. You don't abdicate responsibility. You take ownership for the choices you make.

The Analytic is also methodical and unafraid of numerical conversations. Those don't scare you like they would someone like a Hurdler. You are also open to learning, giving ample thought to planning more than the typical person. If you can find a good system, you will be a good executor of that system. So once you understand what you want to do, you'll be a great executor of it.

Many people who fall into the Analytic category are forced out of their comfort zone as work and life gets busy. If you find yourself in that space where endless research is no longer an option because your family, career, or other obligations do not allow you that flexibility of time, you may need to work on your implementation skills to help you make progress. The good news is that Analytics can make this leap if they refocus their efforts of research and trust other people to help them execute.

WEAKNESSES

Compared to everyone else, Analytics don't abdicate, but they also don't delegate. Rather, you prefer to muscle through things yourself to the point that you end up building your own systems, tracking sheets, and methods. Because this "analysis" phase is rather entertaining and interesting, the Analytic is more comfortable spending time in the review process and may not progress to actual action.

The Analytic is the last person to ask for help. For instance, Ian knows he's capable of working things out for himself. He's smart, after all. But he hasn't committed to a robust set of financial strategies, because he simply doesn't have the time to do that. In addition, Ian doesn't look at financial decisions from a place of opportunity cost. Rather than comparing two strategies and determining that one is better than the other, he'd rather find the perfect solution—which, unfortunately, doesn't always exist.

Because Analytics are so hesitant to ask for help, they are the type of client least likely to seek professional financial advice. And if they do seek help, they tend to come in with their guards up. The process to get them through the Financial Execution Gap is a lot slower because they're so hesitant to make a decision—they'd rather spend time finding the very best solution, and they want to understand things in their totality. While that is admirable, it can be difficult to be a master of every subject, including financial planning.

Does this sound like you? Unless you decide to get a specific degree and delve into a particular subject, you're never going to feel like you know enough. Accepting this about yourself is the first step to moving on and taking action. That's when we can use all of your strengths as well as your weaknesses to help further you toward stress-free financial wellness.

Action Steps: Where Does the Analytic Go from Here?

BUDGET

Budgeting is crucial to finding financial wellness. Typically, as an Analytic, taking inventory of your current financial state is something you have likely already accomplished in the past. If you haven't, do it now using the budget sheet at the back of this chapter, unless you prefer to build your own. As an Analytic, you'll actually enjoy this process, pulling information from everywhere possible and dividing expenses into the categories of fixed and lifestyle expenses, as well as savings. This might be a different lens that you haven't looked through before, so really give thought to what's going on with your spending. Maybe you missed some of those components in previous attempts at budgeting.

Once you've completed that, you'll have a clear and concise set of data. Analytics tend to make things more complicated for themselves than necessary, such as creating a complex spreadsheet, but breaking it down into digestible parts will help in progressing more seamlessly on financial decisions. Give my budgeting sheet a try before considering a five-hour process of formatting a great, aesthetically pleasing budget spreadsheet.

Keeping track of your month-to-month spending is easy. Analytics have a great grasp on their spending, so you—if you identify as such—might see things numerically (an advantage). Therefore monitoring your spending and doing a recap on a monthly basis of what you bring in is an enjoyable step.

Track everything that's not a regular expense, such as travel, holiday gifts, and property tax. If it's not paid on a monthly basis, just take a view of those things from an average monthly cost and put that into the budget so it's easier to make decisions based on a holistic cash flow. As an Analytic, you're someone we can ask that of, whereas a Capable Student or a Hurdler might have a hard time with that ask.

While you probably have a good idea of your spending habits, take stock again. You may have a routine system in place, such as paying bills on a certain day or examining your numbers every Monday. And although you might be conscious of what's going out of your account, executing on the next level is where you stumble, so try not to spend too much unnecessary time in the research phase.

It may take a few tries, but stick with it. The best opportunity for the Analytic is to keep trying and stay open-minded to finding a good approach that works, walking from start to finish through this process to see if it helps you tighten up that decision-making timeline.

For instance, I know an Analytic who created a spreadsheet system that tracks his entire net worth. He is proud of his complex creation. The collection of spreadsheets probably took him fifteen hours—when there are plenty of online tools that could have achieved the same result, and it would have been a dynamic one he wouldn't have to update. Therein lies a problem. He actually enjoys doing these types of things for himself. He may complain about it, but at heart, his passion is the process. And eventually being able to view his work as a comprehensive report on paper brings him joy.

Remember that the purpose of this book and self-identification of your FIN type is to help you take action and shorten the Financial Execution Gap. We are here because something has been holding you and your financial plan back; working through a new mindset and process may help move the needle.

SET GOALS AND BUILD A PLAN

Setting goals and building a plan around them might be different and more unnatural for Analytics like you who'd rather start with facts. It's best to begin by setting goals, as opposed to doing research, which is how many Analytics fall into that Financial Execution Gap. Setting your goals first and then researching based on those goals will get Analytics to their goals more efficiently.

Up to this point, you may have approached financial decision-making based on ideas you have read about or heard and then researching on them. For example, if you hear of an interesting loophole in the tax code, you might want to follow that through to determine if you should execute on that. Let's approach this a bit differently. To begin building a financial plan that you can truly progress with, start with goals in mind.

For example, Ian can begin by identifying if there's anything long-term that's really important to him, including a career change, buying a house, getting married, and/or starting a family. Is it important for him to buy a rental property? Does he want to start his own company? What are the long-term goals for Ian? Will he want to provide for his parents as they get older? Analytics tend to start much smaller, with a micro view of things, so for this exercise, try to focus on big-picture goals.

Reframe the financial conversation and recognize that this is really about wellness and what's important to you as opposed to just a formula, so you need to identify what you want to go after. Others may start small and go big, while you should strive to begin with loftier goals. Once a large, long-term goal is identified, then it's time to set goals for two-to-three years from now. What needs to happen to get you closer to those big-picture goals?

For example, if you want to own a home and feel that you can do so in the next three years, you should narrow your focus and be more specific, defining the neighborhood and approximate purchase price and down payment required.

With both big-picture and two-to-three-year goals in mind, now you can make decisions around what it takes to progress toward those goals. Continuing with the home purchase goal example, the progress necessary for you to get there is to save and grow resources at a particular rate.

With a clear-cut goal in mind, begin your decision-making process around that goal. You need to calculate all relevant factors. Do you want an emergency fund, too? How much do you want to put down on the house? Once you're clear on those goals, your savings options should be narrowed down so you can better determine a three-year plan that best suits you.

You may conclude that you should invest those dollars in a non-retirement, investment account that has a lower amount of risk. By getting clearer and clearer on your goal, it can be more obvious what choices you have now. This is important because the Analytics' biggest problem is making a decision, procrastinating, and widening the gap.

ANALYTIC'S DECISION-MAKING FUNNEL

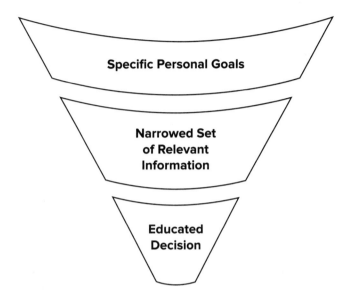

To achieve Ian's broad retirement goal, he should decide if he can save a higher percentage of his income and ask himself how he can invest those dollars properly. If Ian just keeps thinking about making changes and never takes action, he might miss out on years of saving, growing, and building a financial identity.

As an Analytic, you or Ian could find data that supports whatever investment truth you want, but clarifying goals and deciding to start making decisions, one way or another, is a healthier approach to financial wellness than always wondering what you should be thinking about and feeling left behind.

You may prefer reading prospectuses and researching potential tax law changes, but doing so can further delay the decision-making process. Ian wants to feel confident when he eventually executes, and he wants to make sure he's making a decision on purpose, not by default. That's a big mistake Analytics make. They think that they're not making a decision, but are rather postponing that decision so they can be more strategically prepared. But by not making a decision, they're deciding on whatever the default is. No decision equals a decision to do nothing.

Retirement: If you're going to spend your time somewhere, retirement is a good place to utilize your love of research. Look at a retirement model that shows you the impact of your contribution, and make sure you understand both tax and market diversification.

Deciding where to retire is a decision that you'll live with for a long time. Retirement funds need reviewing every year for forty years, and those funds will be distributed over a thirty-or-so-year retirement. But there's a balance between researching responsibly and taking action. Don't wait for perfection, because you'll likely never find an absolutely perfect solution. And if you wait too long into the research phase, you lose benefits such as deferred growth, thus undoing your good intention.

It's easy for an Analytic such as yourself to fall behind if you don't build a plan now to suit your personality and strengths and work around your weaknesses. You know you make decisions by default, so your strategy must now change. For example, you aren't sure if you want to contribute to your 401(k) or do an IRA, because your 401(k) doesn't match. But if you sit on that for two years, you don't serve yourself any better because you didn't save any money. You chose secret option number three, which was to save nothing.

Creating a choice of three possible solutions may make it easier for you to get to the point of decision. Instead of believing there are endless choices, your new plan could be to get your goals down to two or three decisions that can be made immediately. You need to be know that those are the three choices: your 401(k) at work that doesn't match, an IRA, or nothing at all.

For an Analytic, the financial decision-making process is akin to the process of elimination. Sometimes, picking the best decision, not the perfect one, *is* the best decision. So if you know you want to save, and don't want option three, then just pick the one you're the most knowledgeable about.

When the Analytic builds a plan, the key for them is to identify the goals and the decisions to be made, and the best decisions possible under the circumstances. While you may take pleasure in reviewing your plan on a monthly basis, doing so on a quarterly basis could prevent you from kicking the can down the road on any decisions, so that's another consideration. You may be able to see more actual progress quarterly, as well.

LEARN NEW HABITS

So how do you build new habits? You can learn new habits by being open to trying things a little differently. You're good at learning good habits through practice, so taking on some of the easier financial decisions first will help that build-up.

Pinpoint, define, and narrow down the possibilities relevant to you. Focus on having a sensible timeline for making decisions and stick to it. A lot of Analytics will avoid setting the follow up meeting with a financial adviser because they want open-ended time to make a decision. They'd rather research matters for themselves first before handing the wheel over to a professional. Inevitably, the adviser could end up searching for them, taking three or four months to get back in front of clients because Analytics haven't had time to do an infinite amount of research. After all, they have jobs and lives, so they just keep pushing it off.

Be aware of your weakness to stick around in the Financial Execution Gap and take control of it. Otherwise, remember you really are making a decision by not making a decision. Create a decision-making timeline and err on the side of urgency, because your nature will only tell you to continue researching for "a little longer."

For an Analytic to really progress with new financial habits, it's important to understand what the big-picture goals are, have a narrowed set of information on them, and make a decision from there. Don't research how simple IRAs work when what you have available to you is a 401(k). That's what you need to focus on for this period of time in order to make a decision. If the subject is of interest to you, then you can take a class on it in your free time, but don't use it as an excuse to postpone executing on a decision. Build habits by practice, help progress them, and it will get easier to make decisions as you move on.

Setting up your new environment in a healthy way involves accountability. While an Analytic may not need accountability when it comes to saving or budgeting, you'll need a partner or planner to make sure you are making decisions in a timely manner. Find someone who can help you change your research habit to one of proactive nature.

Don't be swayed. Going down the Google black hole will waste precious time. Begin with what's important and follow that.

FOLLOW-THROUGH

For you to follow-through, you must decide to start deciding. Making decisions is key, and progress should be measured based on what you've accomplished, not what you've learned (that will happen inevitably). You need to feel competent enough to make good decisions, but what you really need to measure is how effective you are with follow-through and execution. If you need help, get an adviser or find an accountability partner.

Does the Analytic prefer auto-contributions? You may feel very capable and actually like the idea of going online every month to shift dollars around, but it also puts the pressure on to make more decisions every single month. That could get you stuck. It may be easier for you to do auto-contributions and then review those quarterly or even every six months. By simplifying this particular process, you aren't bogged down with the burden of constant execution and the possibility of delaying execution.

For the highest likelihood of success, Analytics such as yourself require that problems and decisions be simplified and all unnecessary variables be removed, and the only way you will get your needs met is by acknowledging this as a priority. You also need to take a macro view on what's really important to you, which is a step a lot of Analytics skip because you like living in the "now."

Define your future as best as you can. Once you identify your long-term plan, you can build a plan around it. Now that you know your goal, you can decide how much money you can allot to retirement, as opposed to living in a state of eternal options. Now, you can build short-term goals to help execute on those macro visions.

What's going to help you get there? What options are you deciding between?

If you make the decision to work with a financial adviser, let that person know that you're analytical and that you need respectful accountability to make decisions. Lean on the adviser. Financial planners can provide you with research, presenting it to you in a clear and concise way that filters out all of the unnecessary information that's irrelevant to you. As professionals in their field, they can hand you information that saves you hours inside a wormhole—starting something and getting further into it without progress—and they can lead you in the right direction.

One consideration is to opt for a fee-based planner. As an Analytic, you know you could do some of this yourself, but trusting a planner could still be worthwhile. For example, you could technically exercise on your own but maybe a personal trainer will make you get up early every morning and challenge you to work harder than you would on your own, effectively getting you to your goal in record time. You may have a great ab workout routine, but that trainer probably knows many more efficient methods than you. Likewise, working with an adviser doesn't mean you're not smart enough or capable of making a decision. It means that you're wise enough to seek the advice of professionals who will more efficiently guide you there.

You have so many strengths, Analytic. You just need to understand what's important to you so you can use that narrowed set of information that's relevant to your situation and make educated decisions. Since you picked up this book and have read this far, I know you're prioritizing what's important. You know that financial wellness now is essential to a comfortable and stress-free future. So create the funnel of information you need to help you execute and shorten your decision-making timeline.

ANALYTIC Budget Template

FIXED EXPENSES	COST
Mortgage/rent	
Property tax	
HOA/maintenance fee	
Home owner's/renter's insurance	
Utilities	
Cell phone	
Cable/TV/Internet	
Auto payment	
Auto insurance	
Fuel	
Groceries	
Education costs	
Childcare	
Health care costs	
Student loan payments	
Credit card debt payments	
Other debt payments	
Misc.	
Misc.	
Misc.	
TOTAL	

LIFESTYLE EXPENSES	COST
Dining out	
Personal care	
Clothing/dry cleaning	
Hobbies	
Gym membership costs	

LIFESTYLE EXPENSES CONT'D	COST
Membership services	
Household supplies	
Babysitting	
Travel	
Gifts	
Misc.	
Misc.	
Misc.	
TOTAL	

SAVING/FINANCIAL TOOLS	COST
Contributions to savings account	
529/college accounts	
HSA/FSA/DCA	
Non-qualified investment contributions	
Retirement accounts	
Life insurance	
Disability insurance	
Long-term care insurance	
Misc.	
Misc.	
Misc.	
TOTAL	

TOTAL MONTHLY EXPENSES	COST
Monthly take-home income	
Minus fixed expenses	
Minus lifestyle expenses	
Minus saving expenses	
TOTAL UNALLOCATED DOLLARS	

PART III

Find Other FIN Types

Self-information can be overwhelming for some but, I hope, for you it means everything is beginning to make a lot of sense. Did you find your FIN type and get affirmation? Did you feel encouraged knowing there's a word to define exactly how you feel and behave and that there are others experiencing the same obstacles to financial success as you?

Thinking of, talking about, and acknowledging money can often be overwhelming. But it's an important subject, and, frankly, if you don't feel overwhelmed you're in the minority. Most people feel sensitive and as if they're lagging behind and around the subject. Self-information can provide clarity in that sense or it can become more overwhelming because now that you've acknowledged the situation, you're left with the decision to do something about it. Guess what? That's normal.

But remember the pros and cons of your FIN type and how you compare to others. That should provide a sense of relief and encouragement. I also encourage you to talk to a friend, partner, or co-worker about planning to see how they might be approaching it differently than you. The more comfortable you are talking about money, the better relationship you're likely to have with it. When in doubt, just flip to the chapter that best defines you and reiterate those lessons on how to budget, set goals, build a plan, learn new habits, and follow-through on execution.

It all starts with self-information and ends with shortening the Financial Execution Gap. Once you accept your strengths and weaknesses, you know what it is about yourself that you can utilize to further you toward your goals. And you'll know what weaknesses to look out for and how to stay strong during the execution process.

One May Not Define You

Maybe more than one chapter spoke to you. If the FIN Type Quiz revealed that you are between two FIN types, that's normal, too. You may even identify with three FIN types. For example, if you're partially a Capable Student and a Diligent Saver, you might need to spend a little bit more time on education, but you might also need an accountability partner, someone to help you execute faster, since you like to learn all you can before making a decision.

Evaluate where you fall between those two and what components of each of those types speak to you—not because they sound easier, but because they seem more likely to work with your personality and habits as you learn to execute on your finances.

In my practice, I've come across many different combos of FIN types, but I've found that the following are the most common.

Analytic-Implementer

I had to adjust my own approach to finance based on knowing I'm part Implementer and part Analytic. I'm naturally an Analytic—I love doing research, digging deep, and really understanding things.

I would rather research all day long if I had nothing else that was pressing, but life's gotten too complicated to continue like that.

As my life has gotten busier and more complex, I've had to lean more on my Implementer nature, because I can't do it all. I had to face that fact one day. If something's important to you, sometimes you need to delegate some of the smaller items or some of the action items elsewhere. I had to move from a researcher role and into a CEO role of my financial life, delegating all I can so I'm freed up to focus on bigger things. I've leaned into my Implementer side and have found people I appreciate working with and who I feel understand me and are competent in different areas of my life. I allow them to bring me the more narrowed set of information so I can make a decision and have them execute in appropriate situations. I don't have to be the one filling out the paperwork or researching every component of something.

For example, I'm an avid exerciser. I've decided there are a couple of classes I'd like to take, and I work with a trainer now who understands what I'm trying to accomplish. That way, I don't have to plan or think about what I'm doing. I just go there and execute on it, and I let the trainer build my schedule as opposed to me researching to determine the right mixture of classes and the best workout routine for my specific goals. I'm usually coming straight from a meeting, and I don't have a lot of time to mentally shift into that role of thinking through what's going to be the most effective workout for that day.

But when I once had more time, I could actually write out my own workout schedules, and plan it all according to my goals. And I had plenty of room to do that, but that just isn't the case anymore. While some of you may have similar tendencies, you have to move into an Implementer role as life changes and priorities shift.

Capable Student-Implementer

Others may be a mix of Capable Student with a little bit of an Implementer mixed in—they've been self-reliant up to this point. Maybe you've been in school and didn't have a lot of money or resources to work with, so you've had to do everything. But potentially, as life starts to shift, the Capable Student has to learn to lean into an Implementer role. It's challenging for the Capable Student, because this person is so accustomed to doing everything that it's difficult to learn to trust others to do the job right. Life and its accumulating responsibilities transform a person to be more of an Implementer.

I've discovered that many young physicians are great examples of Capable Students. They want to learn, do everything right, and are active participants in their planning, but their jobs don't allow them adequate time to get much accomplished. Leaning into their Implementer tendencies will be beneficial; the conversations will be more specific to the situation. This will lead to decisions and execution by a professional. If you try to build every facet of financial planning into your schedule, you might not get that retirement account set up for two years because you could simply be too overwhelmed with the amount of time that you spend working and the mental pressure that goes into your job.

Hurdler-Implementer

I've also run into Hurdlers who have characteristics of an Implementer in other areas of their lives. Those people might be classified as a Hurdler when it comes to money but when it comes to other things, they're really on top of it. They over-identify with the Hurdler because they feel ignorant when it comes to money. They can't get it right, and it's always been a sore spot, so they're just looking through a negative lens when it comes to money matters. But they have great Implementer tendencies when it comes to their jobs, for example. These people need to work hard to pull the Implementer out of them to make things easier—they just need to find someone else who can tell them what to do, stay on them, give them accountability, and push them into the Implementer role.

When I meet with clients like this I ask permission to hold them accountable to what they say they want to do, and I insist on automatic withdrawals from their accounts for contributions to retirement and in other categories. I make very short deadlines with them, and if I need them to sign paperwork, I'll make rules like a forty-eight-hour deadline. My job as a planner is to push them into the Implementer role and out of the Hurdler role.

Diligent Saver-Analytic

Many engineers, CPAs, and others who are in analytical-type jobs are typically gifted with organized money habits. They would be called Diligent Savers-Analytics. The issues that Diligent Savers-Analytics tend to have is that though they will save plenty of money, the real issue is that they don't look at financial decisions from an opportunity–cost standpoint.

When I work with a client who's a Diligent Saver-Analytic, that person usually wants to prove why something does or doesn't work. They find the research behind things and look for other options. They don't realize, for example, that statistically they'll be better off investing their excess cash in a diversified fashion over time versus stock picking. Sometimes it's not about making the absolutely perfect decision but the best possible decision available within a reasonable timeframe. Otherwise, they'll sit on a lot of cash and that's better than having a saving problem to begin with but it's still not going to help them maximize what they're trying to accomplish.

Relationships

According to a 2015 SunTrust Bank survey of people in a relationship or partnership, finances are the leading cause of relationship stress, with 35 percent of all respondents who are experiencing relationship stress saying money was the primary cause. Nearly half of those aged forty-four to fifty-four with relationship stress say that money is the cause of it all.

If you live with your partner, you may be nodding your head in agreement right now, because it's true. And if money stress has seeped into the relationship, it can affect all other areas of that partnership as well as your own life—your career, self-esteem, and friendships.

It's hard to build good habits and feel great about the financial decisions you make as an individual. And when you try to make those decisions in conjunction with someone else, it can lead to hostility, miscommunication, and a lot of headaches. The problem is that, sometimes, two people speak in very different languages. You may speak as a Diligent Saver, with no idea that your partner is a Hurdler who just doesn't see money the way you do. Or you might be an Implementer, and your partner is an Analytic, and you don't know why it's taking so long to make a decision.

You may speak different languages, but understanding each other's FIN types can help you create common financial identities so you can both have your own financial plan. Every relationship, when it comes to shared money and decision-making roles, can be different. But rarely is it in a relationship's best interest for one person to have complete autonomy over money decisions, while the other person is in the dark. Your financial life together doesn't have to be split 50/50, but it's usually not helpful to completely bifurcate responsibility.

Spouses: A Financial Planner is Cheaper than Therapy

It's prudently important that we take time to learn how to communicate about money in order to ease powerful financial tension in a relationship. The best way to do that is, again, to learn about who you are but to also learn as much as you can about your partner. Are you baffled by the choices that your partner has made financially, or by how rigid they are about money or their debt? Does your partner hound you about the debt you have? Is your partner less concerned about money than you? If you answered yes to any of those, then you and your partner are having a hard time understanding one another and you need to learn each other's language. If you don't have a financial identity as a couple, inevitably there's going to be a presence of tension.

I recommend that you read this book together as a couple—discover both of your FIN types and read your own chapter as well as the one that applies to your partner. Then you can have more perspective about one another and why you operate the way you do, and that can be a conversation starter.

When it comes to partner relationships, you really are capable of talking about money without the conversation becoming unbearably heated. It's true. You both have similar goals and you already know how to communicate well, presumably, except when it comes to money. But it's perfectly normal to prefer an outside moderator to step into this conversation. And guess what? Getting a financial planner to assist is a lot cheaper than therapy. An adviser can walk you through those hard conversations so it's not one of you hounding the other. It's normal to get a third party involved, someone who can save you a lot of grief, heartache, crying, and anger as they help identify what's important to you as a couple and as individuals. If you wouldn't want to be your spouse's personal trainer, you might not want to be their money trainer, either.

BEST PRACTICES FOR A FINANCIAL DISCUSSION

Find Commonality

First and foremost, if you're going to take the time doing something like this, you have to first make sure you have clear goals so you can both focus on what you really want. Take time to understand your own perspective and FIN type, and then partner's, as well. If your goals are the same, it's a lot easier to get to the same destination.

If becoming more financially responsible is the goal for only one of you, then you will inevitably encounter roadblocks. You can also expect friction if your goals are different, or if one goal is less important to one of you than the other. For my clients Seth and Mona, paying for their kids' education is very important to Seth. Mona disagrees. She worked her way through college and feels that that experience has shaped her. Seth wants to provide both undergraduate and graduate help to their kids—that's the life he had and he wants that for his children, too. But they have to find common-ality and compromise somehow—one option could be paying for undergrad and not graduate school, or vice versa. Another compro-mise that could appease them both is to pay for the kids' college but perhaps not their expenses, like rent, food, and utilities—that way, Seth can sleep well knowing their children won't wind up with crippling college debt, and Mona can be more confident that the kids will learn financial responsibility and build character by paying for their own lives. Whatever the disagreement is, working together to identify goals and discuss where things are seen through different lenses is important.

It's normal to disagree sometimes, to be less than 100 percent on the same page with every single goal. But strive for a compromise so you can start progressing.

Divide Responsibilities

Next, decide who's in charge of the money. Do you want decisions to be split between you two 50/50? Will someone take the lead, provided the other person is kept in the loop? Is one of you the appli-cation person who deals with opening accounts and meeting with an adviser, or will you divide those responsibilities? It is less important how these roles are divided, and more important that this is a decision made together along with how communication can be expected.

Be careful not to pigeonhole one partner with all financial responsibilities. Just because your partner minored in business in college doesn't mean they have the energy as a thirty-five-year-old adult with a demanding career to hold down the financial fort at all times. That's like assuming someone who's good at biology should solely handle all family healthcare responsibilities. Don't acciden-tally abdicate financial planning duties on one person just because they're good with numbers. Likewise, it's okay to let your partner know you'd like professional guidance or to do this as a team—be honest about what responsibilities you can and cannot handle. Many partners who are pushed into the money role for the family feel overwhelmed but don't know how to tell their partner that they don't have all the answers.

Be Honest

It's really important to be honest when it comes to money and relationships. Admit what you don't know, your concerns, your goals, your cash flow, and your spending. You can't make real progress with dishonesty or silent dishonesty present. If you're having trouble voicing your concerns aloud or admitting that something that embarrasses you, you may find it beneficial to enlist a financial adviser who can meet with you separately to help educate and walk you through the appropriate steps without embarrassing you. That person can make sure both parties are represented and have a shot at making the good changes you need to make to get you closer to your goals.

Financial Dial: Where Are You?

Partners fall into different categories when it comes to combining finances. Some couples get married or decide to build a life together at a time when there's not a lot going on yet—they're starting fresh. There's little debt and new careers with starting salaries, and so it's easy to combine finances. But also, many people are getting married later in life, bringing with them (good and bad) financial baggage, like credit card debt, student loans, high credit scores, low credit scores, retirement savings, and zero savings. In the latter case, combining finances can take more work.

So it's important to determine where you and your partner are on the finance spectrum. On the left side of the financial dial, you have completely separate finances, while on the right side you've joined up everything: savings, bank accounts, and more. The middle of the dial is the middle ground, where there's at least a joint account present.

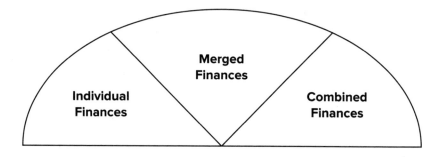

What you have to agree on when you and your partner design your plan is how much money will go into a joint account to pay bills, or who pays for what. Then there should be a discussion around retirement contributions, because if you're planning a life together, the choices that one of you makes around contributing to retirement matters to the other person. You need to set ground rules on debt management, retirement contributions, and you must, at some level, communicate about how filing your taxes separately or together will impact the other person.

If you're on the far left of the dial, know that you can't make 100 percent of your own decisions. You can keep your accounts separate, certainly, and manage things that way, either for the cleanliness of it or for the fact that you are more at ease operating that way. Nothing's wrong with that, but there are decisions, like filing taxes, you should make together.

In the middle of the dial is the middle ground, where a couple has predominantly combined expenses, "merged finances." The majority of your dollars are in a joint account that's used to pay bills or most of your operating costs of living: mortgage or rent, utilities, and groceries. It doesn't have to be based on income—maybe only one of you works but the joint account reflects how much it costs to live your lives together. You make retirement decisions and debt decisions together, but you may have your own savings or checking account for specific purchases or certain accumulation.

At the far right of the dial is the couple with fully combined expenses—there's one savings and one checking account. All decisions are made together under that one account, and there are no dollars that are separated.

A lot of my clients fall somewhere between the first and second category, but not on purpose. For example, two people get married and open a joint account. Maybe one of you forgot about a retirement account you opened years ago. One of the mistakes I see is that retirement accounts might be set up where one person's is aggressive and the other's is conservative, which isn't sensible since they're the same age with the same retirement goal most likely. There's been no communication about how the accounts should be set up, which is an example of why couples need to proactively make decisions together. That couple won't decide every single thing together, and that's okay, but being conscious of retirement allocation as a couple is a goal they should strive for sooner rather than later. It's important to decide on how to handle money as a couple so you're both on the same page.

Common FIN Type Combos

Let's tackle a few different primary financial relationship examples between parents and children, spouses, and roommates, starting with couples.

Couples

IMPLEMENTER + ANALYTIC, JONAH AND BRANDY

My clients, Jonah and Brandy, have been married for eighteen months and they are not ready to start a family yet. He's an Analytic, she's an Implementer. She likes getting information and making a decision on it as swiftly as possible so she can be done with it and move on, whereas he likes to review things. They both work in a field that's somewhat analytical, but they approach things differently—having a financial plan was at top-of-mind for them both. They're in their early thirties, and when it comes to finances, they're on top of it for the most part, making particularly good retirement contribution decisions thus far. And they're fairly clear on how much they spend on a monthly basis.

They have a lot going on, but Jonah's analytical nature is starting to slow down decision-making. They've mostly combined finances but haven't looked at their retirement accounts to ensure they're both allocated correctly and aligned toward their combined goals.

Brandy proactively purchased life insurance and disability insurance when she was single because it made sense to her to have that in place, but Jonah hasn't done that yet. These two have to get each other up to speed and start making those bigger decisions together that will impact one another.

Jonah set up a brokerage account years ago, making small contributions toward it thus far—he's just playing around basically. But Brandy isn't keen on that strategy, preferring instead to find a plan with more purpose behind it than simply paying for stocks they know relatively little about.

The first thing I instructed them do was to go through their goals together. They'd never truly done that. Though they'd purchased a home and discussed wanting kids, they hadn't talked about what their lives together looked like from a career standpoint, where their expectations center around income. We spent time on that since Jonah, the Analytic, can make a decision with ease if he knows the purpose of that decision.

Throughout the money discussions, Jonah was frustrated with Brandy because she wanted to move faster than he was willing to execute. So to speed things up, I tried to help him focus on having a narrow set of information relevant to him to make those decisions easier.

For Brandy, the Implementer, it was important that she take the time to review those things, including plans she already had in place. For instance, the disability insurance she had put in place five years ago was much smaller than she currently needs as it was based on her income several years ago. It was important to force her to take time and examine what's changed.

Jonah and Brandy essentially need to understand their goals and spend more time on them together. They decided to have timelines in place that made sense for both of them. So while Brandy's ready to make decisions the second something makes sense, they decided that to have a seven-day timeline for every decision—seven days to think, then decide on the deadline day. This gives Jonah time to research, review, and ponder, while also providing him with a sense of urgency he didn't have before. He can still learn more if he wants to do that in his free time, but not on their watch as a couple—the research phase should no longer prohibit Jonah and Brandy from taking action.

HURDLER + DILIGENT SAVER, TYLER AND JESSIE

When I met Tyler and Jessie, they were engaged but hadn't yet married, and I met with them individually. At that point the two hadn't decided to have those financial conversations together yet, so both parties were more comfortable initially with getting financial advisers separately. While digging into their situation, it was revealed to me that Jessie had a significant amount of debt she'd yet to disclose to her fiancé. It was important to her to get her situation in order quickly and to be honest with him soon, but she didn't know how to bring it up.

She's never really taken a lot of time to think through her finances. For Jessie, it's simply not been a priority—it's not what she wants to spend her time doing. Money talk overwhelms her, causes her stress, and makes her feel bad about how much things will cost one day, like a wedding and children. But she's realized it's a conversation she needs to start having, first with herself, but, as one would expect, there's anxiety surrounding her as she approaches the subject.

Tyler is a cut-and-dry decent saver. Part of that is owed to him setting up accounts when he was young, where he'd deposit $100 a month, increasing that amount as he's gotten older. But he's stockpiling the cash rather than strategizing about his plan. He doesn't spend a lot of money because he doesn't really need to.

For Tyler, having debt is a baffling concept. It's simply not part of his lingo, and he sees things in very black-and-white terms when it comes to money. For each of them, it's first and foremost important for them to respect that the other has a very different approach to money. It's not simple. They must take the time to realize that they just see things through a different paradigm.

As a Hurdler, Jessie may find that money isn't a fun conversation, but reality is setting in now. Normally, if she has extra money, she spends it, but she knows that doesn't make her feel great, though it never really bothered her in the past. But the stakes are higher now. She knows her spending had gotten out of control and now she wants to focus on having a life, one day having a marriage, a home, and kids. And she doesn't want to disappoint her fiancé.

Two things need to happen with Tyler and Jessie. One, as we discussed, is that they need to understand and respect each other. They need to get very clear on what their goals are so that it's important to them both. And this couple needs to decide how they'd like to combine finances when it comes to short-term expenses, like a wedding, and also when it comes to long-term expenses, like buying a house, having kids, or making retirement contributions.

Communication is key for Tyler and Jessie. They have to be open about finances in order for them to make sound decisions and lovingly hold each other accountable. With this particular combo of FIN types, it could be beneficial to bring in a third party to help them accomplish their goals, since they're very much speaking two different languages when it comes to money. A financial adviser can keep things low-stress, asking questions to find out what's going on while remaining nonjudgmental. Judgment is what will shut Jessie down completely and prevent her from making progress.

Tyler and Jessie must work on building an identity together, since he, as a Diligent Saver, might be prone to keeping his money separate since she's not great at saving. For example, if she's not contributing to a 401(k) and foregoing a 3 percent match because she's paying down debt, and he's contributing 8 percent to his 401(k) with a 2 percent match, there's some alignment that can happen to benefit them as a couple who, presumably, intend to grow old together.

Communication will benefit them at every turn, especially when it comes to helping their joint net worth. In this case, they decided he would start paying the $200 cable bill, and she signed up for her 401(k) match, given that paying the cable bill was removed from her plate. Now they've started growing resources for retirement together.

The big theme for Tyler and Jessie is that they need quarterly meetings and small habits to change. Tyler has to focus on what he can do to be more strategic in his plan, while Jessie is focused on facing financial responsibility. Instead of staying focused on what one person is doing wrong, they're turning to each other and making their life together the center of attention.

Tyler and Jessie have officially arrived at the middle of the dial. Now, they have a joint account from which they pay their bills, because they spent that time budgeting and learning what it costs to live their life together. Then they had to start working on credit scores to prepare for buying a house. He agreed to take on more bills to help her get her debt down, and they're still in their quarterly meetings to make sure they stay on track. Falling into old habits can happen easily without proper accountability. And having a financial adviser is great intervention, helping them to avoid hostility. Because they've taken that approach, they're building a great financial identity together based on their combined efforts to make things better.

ANALYTIC-CUM-IMPLEMENTER + IMPLEMENTER, JORDAN AND MIKE

Jordan and Mike are presently both Implementers, but Jordan was always an Analytic. Because of her growing career and responsibilities, she's had to lean into an Implementer role more and more in most areas of her life, though her Analytic side shows sometimes when it comes to money.

Both were successful in their careers. They are also very focused on making great financial decisions. They've been married for a few years and work really hard in equally demanding jobs. Mike, an Implementer through and through, does a great job of getting things done. He manages a lot of people, so he's a big fan of delegating. He'd rather pay for good service to get things done rather than adding to his already-overflowing plate.

An Analytic at heart, Jordan likes to make conscious decisions, and, actually, she works in a sector of the financial world. Therefore, Mike delegates to Jordan most of their financial responsibilities, assuming she's got it under control due to her day job. But since Jordan is also very busy, carrying that weight is overwhelming at times. For her, it's frustrating when Mike constantly questions if she's done this or that yet—it feels as though she's getting micromanaged by her own partner.

But the two have a lot going for them. They're accustomed to getting things done and have high expectations for their life as a couple. It would be helpful for Mike, as an Implementer, to be more involved and to make sure he's not taking advantage of Jordan's career in finance as a reason to push this responsibility to her solely. She doesn't want to sit in the driver's seat at all times, but she does want to be a partner in the decision-making and goal-setting.

In their case, it was worthwhile to meet with an advisor so they could move faster. They're both organized, and they both have good assistants that can get all of their details over to their adviser, who immediately began organizing a plan. Jordan, the Analytic, helped a lot, spending time to send over the appropriate data. The adviser stepped in by helping them to clearly set goals, understand what's going on, and take some of the responsibility off their plates. As a newbie Implementer, Jordan was great about delegating that, because she knew it would otherwise fall through the cracks at some point. She works twelve hours a day, so when things did fall through the cracks, there was palpable hostility between Mike and her. She knows it's in their best interest to let a professional oversee things and consequently remove tension from their relationship.

Despite the fact that they're both wildly capable, there's still great benefit in getting someone else in there to ultimately take responsibility of those details and guide them, leaving them to do what they do best.

CAPABLE STUDENT + CAPABLE STUDENT, COLIN AND CARLA

Colin and Carla are similar when it comes to finance, though Colin is more obviously a Capable Student. Colin is a doctor, while Carla is a stay-at-home mom. He's a few years into his practice and really wants to do the right thing when it comes to money—he's a Capable Student to the core. She wants to make smart decisions, too, and realizes that neither of them have a lot of financial background. It's all new to them, but they're eager to learn.

Colin has a demanding job, so that's why they decided that she, a former journalist, would stay at home and manage the kids and household. It was the best transition for their family—and it's his income they've really depended on. Carla wants to keep them on track with their life goals and be there for the kids, so she's on board with the arrangement.

They want to send their kids to good schools, travel, and buy a forever home (they own a home now, but it's temporary in their eyes). So they have clear goals—they just need to get on track financially.

Colin is the one who's proactively met with financial advisers, but Carla is the one who actually pays most of the bills—she thinks of herself as the household manager, or treasurer. While they thought they were good at having conversations surrounding money, they hadn't thought through everything. For instance, only Colin had life insurance in place through his company. They'd read somewhere that because she didn't work, she couldn't have it, but didn't think about it. Colin can only do his demanding job because Carla's at home with two kids running the household. If something were to happen to her, it would be a mess.

Similarly, Colin didn't have disability insurance, even though he's the primary earner. Carla has been out of the workforce for four years, so it wouldn't be easy for her to jump back in if something were to happen to him. And living off of half his income wouldn't work with their present life and future goals.

Those are small things that may seem obvious but can somehow get lost in the shuffle of a busy life. They had stopped communicating as much and were trying to bifurcate things, which wasn't working. Colin and Carla were seemingly leading different lives throughout the day. They weren't communicating quite enough, so making decisions together became harder to do without those cohesive conversations.

When I came into the picture, I was able to help them verbalize their clarity on short-term goals. He was unaware of how much it costs to live their life and didn't realize how much of his paycheck was used for that every month. Going through their budget together was a healthy exercise for them, as they were able to get clarity on the comings and goings, and they got a handle on the excess available for investment.

Colin and Carla also needed to get more educated on different components of their plan, like risk management, actions surrounding saving for their kids' futures, and retirement. Getting on the same page is key, since it seemed like their lives began operating in a parallel sense, with little time taken to catch up with each other and really discuss their situation. Now they are no longer trying to divide and conquer, but are rather strategizing and executing together.

Since they're both Capable Students, theirs is a case of the blind leading the blind. They may have the best of intentions, however they have to take the time to strategize, connect strategy to their goals, and get things accomplished through execution.

CAPABLE STUDENT + DILIGENT SAVER, CURTIS AND JODI

Curtis is a Capable Student client who's married to Jodi, a Diligent Saver. They both have great jobs—she's a nurse practitioner and he's a lawyer. They've reached the point in their lives where they're having kids and trying to buy a house. While Curtis and Jodi work to discover their financial identity, they've had conversations and realized their different approaches to money. She's never had an issue with saving money. She has always viewed financial success based on what's in her emergency fund, what her debt looks like, and if she's living within her means. That's great. Jodi has the right idea, for the most part.

They're both realistic about their income. Curtis wants to figure this out but doesn't have the natural instincts to save. He has some credit card debt and hasn't been fully maximizing his 401(k) match. Curtis wants to do the right thing, so he has hesitated to make any moves at all, knowing he could risk making a wrong decision. That's led him to do very little for the past ten years, a shame since he's worked up a considerably higher income over the past five years—so the stakes are higher now. They could be smartly securing that extra cash rather than pondering where to go from here.

In their dialogue, Jodi's natural gut reaction is to take over. She knows how much they spend on everything and how much comes in. But she has to make sure he's up to speed and confident in the decisions they're making, since he can add a lot of value to that process. He just needs to understand what's going on.

If Curtis feels confident about where the plan is going, it's going to be easier for him to save and implement that plan. That's what's been missing. He's overpaid on his credit cards but not completely. He has contributed to his 410(k) but without fully maximizing the match. He's done some of the basics but hasn't gone all in, because he's not 100 percent sure of the priority or what the right decision would be.

For Curtis and Jodi, there's an opportunity to make sure they're benefitting from her ability to track what they're doing. She's never going to buy a house without a budget. She's realistic when it comes to that, which they'll benefit from. What they have to do now as a couple is take the time to understand their choices, because he's just been living in the idea that there might be a lot of choices he doesn't understand.

Curtis will not slow them down but force them to think through strategies that will help him understand and go into the plan with full force. Jodi just has to give him a chance, realizing his curiosities might help them make more strategic decisions. It's great that she's an incredible saver, but she's not strategic—that's where Curtis, her perfect match if you think about it, comes in.

As a Capable Student, Curtis has tried a lot of strategies. He has an online investment account he's bought stocks in, and he's trying a few new, different things like that. But he's not all in. He doesn't have a good strategy because he needs help. He's smart enough to figure it out on his own, which is why he hasn't asked for help, but he still feels a little lost. Until he feels good about the decisions he needs to make, he's never going to really implement the way he should. This is their chance to take the time to take in their options, build a financial plan together, and maximize and build on their strengths.

HURDLER + ANALYTIC, BRETT AND SABRINA

Brett works in digital marketing and is a Hurdler. His long-term girlfriend, Sabrina, an aerospace engineer, is an Analytic. They shine in their careers, excelling by earning bonuses. But when it comes to financial decisions, for Brett, it just doesn't click. He finds money stressful, and he's already overwhelmed worrying about his mother, who isn't financially stable. As he watches her struggle, he knows there's a price to pay for living life oblivious to planning for the future. Instead of making preparations, he's enjoyed nice trips and the everyday motto that "You only live once." But he knows that's an excuse and changes need to be made. He just doesn't know how to make them happen yet.

As long-term concerns settle in, Brett has watched friends buy their first homes. Meanwhile, he's not in a position to get his dream home just yet, despite making great money in his career. He has nothing to show for his success, and he's become embarrassed about it.

Sabrina, on the other hand, seems to have it together. She is financially aware and asks questions about what he does with his bonuses that he can't answer. He tends to pay for their trips because it seems easier. Brett doesn't think about it but he has a lot of credit card debt. They've discussed the future, but the stress of that for him has led to fights.

As an Analytic, Sabrina wants to approach their situation from every angle, asking more questions than the average person, which makes Brett closed off and full of anxiety. What she struggles with is that she's over-analyzed finance how-tos. She attends seminars offered at work, reads books, and has conversations with friends who've done smart financial things. She researches online and has read numerous articles on how to approach things like savings and retirement.

The problem is that she's saved some money but without actually building a strategy around it and she's drowning in the research she loves to do and needs a lifeline. It frustrates her that she doesn't have much to show for her work, but it's hard for her to make a commitment when she's unsure of which decision would be the best possible one.

Meanwhile, Brett has nothing to show either because it's not been something he feels like putting his energy into. He wants to spend as little time as possible talking about money, so this couple really needed and benefitted from my intervention—otherwise, their financial conversations would be ongoing misunderstandings ending in arguments. Leaving a couple like this to have open-ended discussions about money can be futile.

I'd recommend a couple like this to take bite-sized pieces and systematic approaches to things, calling in third-party guidance to help them execute. He can't understand why she wants to think about these things, while she is baffled that he won't acknowledge that money needs to be figured out. An adviser will help them find common ground.

Parents + Kids

DOES THE APPLE FALL FAR FROM THE TREE?

In my experience, you learn most of your habits—good or bad—from your parents. Usually, one of the first people you turn to when making a big decision is your mom or dad. But there are a few things to acknowledge both in what you learned and how you seek advice.

Recognize that your parents are different people from a different generation with a different set of opportunities. They may have always paid off their credit cards, or maybe they never had to get one to begin with. Maybe they didn't spend 25 percent of their earnings on travel. Perhaps they set aside a certain amount of money for emergencies, paid their taxes on time, contributed to retirement accounts, and responsibly put documents in place, like wills and trusts. They may have even saved money for education.

Now you might have a desire to understand their decisions and study their beginnings. You ask questions, curious about what they wish they'd done more of or what they're glad they got accomplished. There may be a lot of positive things to learn from your parents and perhaps they've instilled some of those good behaviors in you. Some of those include setting aside money, opening a bank account, and not being afraid to understand how compound growth works.

If you have any of those positives from your family, that can be a gift not everyone acquires. But it's crucial that you acknowledge that some of their decisions were imperfect. Realize that you're not doomed just because you never achieved their financial successes. You can learn from their example of what not to do, as well.

RECONSIDERING RETIREMENT OPTIONS

Not everyone was blessed with an innate ability to make good financial decisions. For example, some parents were not diligent in saving for retirement, and that may be a concern. *You* may be their retirement plan.

Potentially, you may have parents who put money into one or two big stocks, and when the stock market crashed in 2008 they lost a significant amount of money they couldn't recover. If all of their resources were in the stock market and they were retired in 2008, they were forced to take money out in a down market. By selling in a down market, it makes it almost impossible to truly recover at that stage in life when you're no longer contributing. Maybe they didn't have disability insurance and something happened and they couldn't work for a period of time. You saw the repercussions of what that does for a family when you don't have a good backup plan in place.

YOUR FUTURE IS YOUR OWN

You also must acknowledge that what works for one generation can't always be applied to another. If your parents bought life insurance when they had kids, but they had kids at age twenty-one, it may not be fair to compare that to your situation now, a twenty-eight-year-old single person. Maybe you want kids in a few years, but it's not realistic right now. That doesn't necessarily mean you get to delay that decision because health is still a big factor—your health can change a lot between twenty-one and thirty-five, which can impact insurability.

It's likely that even if your parents had student loans, they didn't have to face the same kind of debt that graduates have to deal with today. They may have also lived in a place where housing prices were different, and they've lived in the same house now for forty years.

Maybe homeownership was important to them, whereas it's not quite as important to you, depending on your city or circumstance. And paying for a college education for theoretical children five or fifteen years from now is very different than a state school ten or fifteen years ago.

Recreating your parents' lives and trying to make the same kinds of smart decisions may not be realistic now. In 2018, it's common to have a cell phone bill as well as an Internet bill, which can be an added $250 a month, and that cost simply didn't exist in 1985. These are real differences when you graduate from college and your income is $30-$40,000. It's okay to acknowledge that the things that worked out for one generation won't necessarily translate to this one.

Let's take a common example: Some grandparents and parents encourage their kids and grandkids to open up CDs, or certificates of deposit. A CD is not good or bad however, that is not the question. When your parents were younger, they might have had CDs in the 1980s that were paying a 10 to 15 percent rate. Today, those might be paying less than 1 percent. The times are dictated by a different set of circumstances. That requires evaluations that are tailored to each individual.

When it comes to advice, you have to dig deeper than the surface level and try to make good decisions based on your personal goals and what you have to work with at this particular time in your life.

TAKE RESPONSIBILITY

Also, if you're someone who's reliant on your parents for guidance, it's crucial to make sure that you're making your own financial decisions. Don't place blame your financial ignorance or short-fallings on your parents. It's not fair to them, and it's not fair to yourself to abdicate that responsibility. I've seen parents set up retirement accounts for their kids, which is an act of kindness and helpfulness, but they can be too conservative. It might reflect your risk tolerance, or it might reflect theirs. Make sure you take some financial ownership and look at everything based on what's important to you and what you are trying to accomplish and not put all of the responsibility on a generous parent.

Another common assumption: though clients don't ask their parents this directly, however they assume that if they were disabled, their parents would be able to take care of them. While I'm sure most parents don't want to leave their children out in the cold, that's not really a fair assumption unless you've had a clear conversation with them and they've confirmed that they have ample resources to provide both their retirement for them and care for you. At some point, you have to "adult" a little and take on risk management to protect your income.

Often, parents co-sign on loans, but it's important to have the uncomfortable conversation of life insurance. So when you ask a parent to co-sign, consider having private life insurance of your own. If something happens to you, they'd be stuck paying off your $100,000 graduate degree. That's something no one wants to consider, and parents definitely do not want to think about that kind of thing, but it's important that you take a good proactive financial approach in every possible way.

Don't forget that every child–parent relationship is different. Some parents are wildly generous and can provide help with down payments on a home. It's crucial though that the child understands what that means, what the tax implications are, and that you still strive to build good habits.

Some feel confident that their parents will leave them a good sum of money, that they're bound to have a good inheritance. They use that as an excuse to neglect retirement savings, choosing instead to prioritize their spending differently. If it has not been clearly discussed with your family and written into proper estate planning, don't make that gamble. Don't bet your entire financial plan based on what you assume someone else is going to do for you.

But maybe your parents have never had the means to offer you help, and for many that can mean two things: (1) as an adult, you've either spent too frivolously because you went without as a child, and that's something you may feel ready to address now by building better habits, or (2) you're hyper aware of your spending since you know there's no plan B. That also means that maybe you've considered having to help your parents out at some point down the road if you're not already doing so. Have that conversation with them now about what they have saved thus far, if they've been able to save at all, so you have a realistic view of what's going on with their savings and debt. Then you'll be clear on what that commitment might be if that's important to you.

Whether you are a parent or a child reading this, remember that, like most things, whoever you are, most of our suggestions for planning begin with goals and communication. A lot of parents assume they know their kids well, when they may not actually know their goals. It's worth asking, or it's worth having someone else help to start that conversation.

Roommates

So, how do you live with someone you're not romantically involved with or related to?

Most likely, you're not combining finances. Most rooming situations are temporary, so there's a layer of complexity that isn't there. Still, it can be trying to say the least. There are things that should be discussed so as to avoid discomfort caused by the lack of communication.

Most individuals come from different backgrounds. Potentially, you're splitting utilities with someone who's grown up with every premium channel on cable, while your budget is not one that can handle that expense. The key is to address finances, bills, and utilities early on, and to be aware of the fact that people view money differently.

Many of my clients discover that their roommates make a lot of money or have parents who supplement their income. It's not easy to live with someone who always wants to order takeout but casually needs you to spot them like it's no big deal. It may not seem like an issue to them, but $50 later, your budget for the next few days is gone, all because your roommate simply didn't recognize that you're struggling a little more. Maybe they forget to pay you back, and then it can be awkward to bring it up again—no one likes admitting they're broke—but you also don't want to wind up blowing your paycheck on someone else's takeout habits.

There are also clients whose roommates expect to hire a housekeeper, because that's how they were raised. But for many, that's too expensive and an absolute no-go. So how do you initiate those conversations? The key is to know your budget, be clear, and ask questions before you move in together.

There's always room for compromise. Maybe you can split the cable differently if it's not a necessity for you, but your roommate would then have to be okay with knowing you'll probably wind up watching it here and there. It's just not your choice to have it in the first place. Or maybe there's a cost difference in room sizes, which could be a good solution for you. Most conflicts are solved by communication—and earlier rather than later. And you may find that your roommate wants to have that conversation too—it's just that it can be awkward to bring up.

Also remember that most roommate situations aren't forever. Nothing is forever, and you can always find a different solution. Be clear on what your budget is and the goals that are important to you, and attempt to make it work. You may find you're living with a Hurdler who's unaware of how much they're spending. That person may appreciate the realization that they're spending $200 a month on takeout.

Communication helps you understand what people are focused on but just know that tension is normal. There will always be issues when it comes to making financial decisions, no matter what type of relationship you're involved in. If you understand what your goals are, it'll be easier to factor those complications into your financial plan.

Keep in mind that some people are positive financial influences, while others aren't, so stick to your plan no matter what. Whether your influences have student loans, stocks they've had since birth, or parents who help support them, don't feel badly. At the end of the day, you must make decisions that progress you financially—that you can control.

CONCLUSION

Nurture Your Financial Health

When it comes to financial decision-making, try to separate the unpleasant chores of planning, like filing your taxes, to more encouraging financial responsibilities that will move you into a wellness space. It's an area that needs nurturing, so build a lifelong commitment to financial health. That starts by understanding where you are, who you are, and where you're going, both short and long term.

If you haven't had success in financial planning before, you are not alone! Perhaps your approach was too generic.

Not every human in the world is prescribed the same prescription for the same ailment. Some enjoy swimming as exercise, others don't. Some people are runners, while others have bad knees. Some may need to take a low-impact approach. That's okay—whatever works for you is what you have to execute on. A lot of things in life are based in discipline and goal oriented, including financial success.

Financial journeys are unique and you have to make sure you're on your own path and journey. Hopefully, by identifying who you are—or which two or three FIN type you fit into—you'll have a clear idea of how to build out a financial plan. The most important thing you can do is close that Financial Action Gap and actually implement things that can help you get closer to and conquer your goals.

Whoever you are—whether you're a Diligent Saver, Implementer, Capable Student, Hurdler, or Analytic, or a combination of different FIN types—finding your FIN type should help you have a better follow-through success rate. From here, you have the tools to lead a more stress-free life and achieve financial wellness. Build the best process that works for you, and stay focused, energized, and conscious of the choices you're making.

You don't need a master's degree in finance to build a great personal financial life. And if you do happen to have a finance degree, that doesn't mean you have all the answers. Financial success isn't about perfection—it's about progress, continual progress. Stay the course, because, no matter who you are, with this book and these tools, you'll be capable of taking control of your financial life and accomplishing financial wellness.